Showmanship for Presenters:

49 Proven Training Techniques
from Professional Performers

by Dave Arch

with an introduction by Bob Pike

Creative Training Techniques
Press

Jossey-Bass
Pfeiffer
San Francisco

Printed in the United States of America

Published by

350 Sansome Street, 5th Floor
San Francisco, California 94104-1342
(415) 433-1740; Fax (415) 433-0499
(800) 274-4434; Fax (800) 569-0443

www.pfeiffer.com

Printing   10   9   8   7   6   5   4   3   2   1

 This book is printed on acid-free, recycled stock that meets or exceeds the minimum GPO and EPA requirements for recycled paper.

Thank you
to
Bob Pike,
a true training visionary
in a world with too few dreams.

Other Products by the Author

Techniques and Tricks for Trainers (two-day seminar)

Tricks for Trainers, Volume 1

Tricks for Trainers, Volume 2

First Impressions/Lasting Impressions

Trainer Bingo

Contents

Introduction by Bob Pike, C.S.P

We live in a world of entertainment. We're constantly bombarded and enticed by a myriad of media formats vying for our attention, interest, belief, commitment, and of course, money.

In June of 1995 my daughter Rebecca went to the National Junior College Speech Competition in San Francisco. I arranged my business schedule so that I could be there to encourage her. We went to lunch before her competitions began. During lunch, she asked if I'd listen to one of her speeches. When I asked how long it would take, she said, "It'll only take eight minutes. No speech takes over eight minutes. Television programs never go more than eight minutes without a commercial break." I thought to myself, "Out of the mouths of babes..." (Well, she's not a baby, certainly, but young compared to me.)

What her remarks reminded me of was that media has shaped our lives. Television doesn't take a commercial break every eight minutes because our attention spans are only that long, but perhaps our attention spans shrunk because we've watched so much television that we expect to focus for no longer than eight minutes. And some say the volume is pumped up during commercials because viewers may leave the room during them!

So, what does this have to do with you and me and the world of training? We need to recognize that audiences today are different from audiences of a generation ago. They might not expect anything radically different in the classroom or other presentation environments, but they probably respond more positively if you offer something new.

And that leads to the focus of this book — examining the tools techniques used by master performers from various media to capture the attention, interest, imagination, and hearts of audiences throughout the decades. In these pages you'll explore the nuances and facets that make these performers so effective.

Johnny Carson was effective, so are Jerry Seinfeld and Tim Allen. Yet each of these individuals has his own style. Likewise, you and I don't have to be clones of each other to be effective. Each of us brings our own style to the platform, and this book describes how. For instance, it outlines the master's use of the stage and platform. Are we aware, as trainers, of how to properly stage everything we do? Of how to put everything in it's proper light to maximize the effectiveness of the presentation? Of the importance of managing the presentation from before the audience enters until the last participant exits?

It's not that we want the staging to steal the show...we don't. We want it to be as subtle as the frame surrounding a masterpiece — it's purpose being to properly frame the masterpiece, not to call attention to itself. Proper staging helps create the impact we want.

The principles of master performers have equal value for us. Unique methods for developing segments of material, creating a flow, changing the pace, and ensuring variety have high value in the arena of business presentations. When was the last time you tried a new approach in your repertoire? Do we stick to the tried and true (or even *not* so true) merely because it's comfortable?

Then there are the tools of master performers — the planned spontaneity, the use of conflict to create drama (and 30 minutes later, a satisfying resolution), the use of music to create a mood. Remember the opening scenes of *Psycho, The Sound of Music, Star Wars,* or *The Lion King*? Imagine changing the musical sound tracks — it wouldn't work, would it? I've found a dozen ways to improve my presentations using new and different "tools" — and you can, too.

And finally, the audience itself. Anyone who's been in a play more than one night can tell you how different audiences can be. Does it make a difference when the opening-night house is "stocked" with every friend and family member the cast can squeeze in the auditorium, and the next night, the theater's half full? It can and often does — unless we know how to read the audience and flex our presentation to respond to the audience we actually have in front of us, not the one we'd like to have.

You're about to go backstage and learn the secrets of master performers. As you study these tricks and tips, remember this important discussion: In business presentations (especially in training) our goal is to empower people to be more effective because of what we share. Our purpose must be to empower, not simply impress. Use these tools to empower your audiences, and you'll be well on your way to being a master performer yourself!

HOW TO USE THIS BOOK

A collection of essays examining 49 principles of showmanship, this book brings to a conscious level proven techniques used by famous entertainers. It then transports those techniques right into the training room!

Showmanship for Presenters contains three major sections. The first emphasizes showmanship techniques that apply to the presenter. The second applies additional showmanship principles to the presentation. And the final section examines the techniques that apply to the participants.

If you choose to read the book from cover to cover, you'll find that each chapter builds on the previous ones, creating a logical flow. By using the Contents section, however, you can select any essay of immediate interest. Then, by watching for the bold word(s) in each essay, you'll be directed to other chapters with complementary themes. You can read the entire book in this non-linear manner.

As an adventure in self-discovery, try videotaping your favorite late-night talk show. Then turn to the back of this book, where *The Late-Night Talk Show Training Guide* will help you transform your tape into a training video. By completing the suggested exercises and answering the thought-provoking questions, you can examine and experience all 49 techniques of showmanship!

No matter how you choose to explore the contents of this book, your greatest thrill will come when you first try these time-tested techniques in your own training room. Then you'll discover what professional performers have known for generations—the power of showmanship!

INTRODUCTION

Showmanship is the art of making the ordinary extraordinary.

Showmanship is all around us. Advertisers make ordinary soap, toothpaste, and deodorant seem extraordinary so we'll buy specific brands. Talk-show hosts take ordinary people and make them appear extraordinary so we'll watch their shows. Trainers make ordinary content seem extraordinary to help participants learn. And no matter what the application, the principles of showmanship remain the same.

If I took the world's largest diamond to a training session to show my participants, I probably wouldn't carry it in my pocket. It undoubtedly would be contained in a box or a velvet bag. Before revealing the diamond, I'd set the stage by describing to the participants what they were about to see—giving them enough information to appreciate what I was about to show them. Finally, I'd slowly remove the diamond from its container, hold it up high, look at it, point at it, move it so its many facets caught the light, and then say something like, "Isn't it unbelievable?!"

Should such treatment be reserved for the world's largest diamond? No!

Showmanship is taking the qualities of presentation usually reserved for the uncommon and using them with the common.

This book identifies 49 techniques of showmanship, then describes how to apply them to your training—turning the ordinary into the extraordinary!

It all begins with you...showmanship always begins with the trainer. And so does the first section of this book!

THE PRESENTER

PERSONALITY

-The Indispensable-

Why do some people prefer one comedian over another? Don't all comedians tell jokes? Likewise, why do some prefer one late-night talk show over another? Don't all talk shows feature a host, guests, monologues, and music? And how about singers? Don't they all sing songs? And trainers? They all present content, right? *Personality* makes the difference!

In the case of a singer, the singer finds a song and processes it through his or her personality, singing it in a manner only that person could.

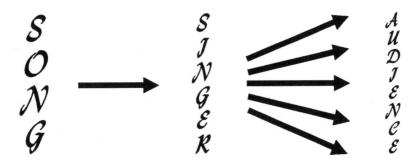

The singer literally shares a part of him- or herself with the audience. When the process works as it should, it's magical! An audience knows when it's happening.

An audience also knows when it's *not* happening. In this sad scenario, the singer sings the song in a technically perfect, albeit mechanical, manner. Or worse yet, the singer tries to sing it just like another singer has performed it. Instead of sharing him- or herself with the audience, the singer hides behind the song. Ultimately, the performance fails to satisfy the listeners.

For several evenings, focus on the musical-guest portion of a late-night talk show. See if you can distinguish between singers who share themselves with the audience and those who merely sing their songs. Once you understand the concept of singers really sharing themselves with the audience, the difference isn't hard to detect.

With an understanding of the process, we can now change the words to *joke, comedian,* and *audience,* and the process remains the same.

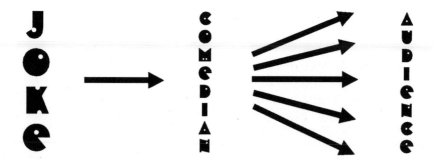

If we use the words *magic trick, magician,* and *audience,* the process is unaffected.

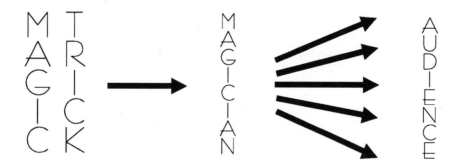

The words *content, trainer,* and *participant*s don't change the process, either.

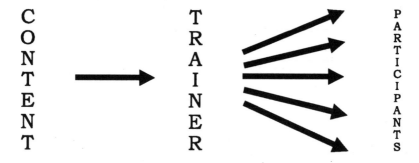

Training is a dynamic form of self-expression. It's not difficult to understand why a trainer with an uninteresting/unlikable personality will have great difficulty presenting any content in an interesting manner. Or why one with an interesting/likable personality will have little difficulty presenting any content in an interesting manner. The difference is the trainer! No high-tech training system could ever compete with or replace a knowledgeable trainer with an interesting personality.

Now for the good news! I've never met a trainer yet who didn't have some characteristics or personality traits that others would find interesting. Sometimes it's a special talent, hobby, interest, or past experience. Sometimes it's a difficulty the trainer has overcome or an admirable character strength. Many trainers, however, take these aspects of their personality for granted; they don't capitalize on their most interesting/likable qualities or focus on their **character development.** Still others are afraid of **vulnerability** and continue to hide their strengths—presenting material but never sharing themselves with their participants. As your own training increasingly becomes a form of self-expression, both you and your participants will notice the difference.

What would others find interesting/likable about you?
The next chapter will help you uncover some answers.

CHARACTER DEVELOPMENT

-Emphasizing Your Strengths-

What's your favorite television sitcom? In the space below, list the leading character's personality qualities. Is that character extroverted or introverted? A "people" person? Into details? Usually, sitcom characters are well defined—often to the point of exaggeration.

_____

_____

_____

_____

Now, describe your favorite late-night talk-show host's personality. What's s/he like? Who's s/he most like of the people you know?

_____

_____

_____

_____

In each of these cases, you weren't trying to describe the real person; you were describing the character that the performer plays on television. You were describing that individual's *persona*.

Although the best talk-show hosts play themselves, even they don't show all of themselves. These performers have chosen the qualities of their **personality** that audiences respond to best and have accentuated these traits. Each has many personal facets that no audience will ever get a chance to see.

A classic example involves a late-night host whose onstage humor leaned toward the sarcastic—undoubtedly an extension of who that individual is. When the audience began responding negatively to that aspect of the host's delivery, however, s/he chose to tone it down. Without its negative edge, the host's humor became much more enjoyable—the audience could finally quit feeling sorry for the guests! Although this performer still may be fairly sarcastic off-stage, s/he has tempered the degree to which this trait is shown to audiences.

Whenever we, as trainers, work with participants, we also are "in character." Although we aren't presenting a character completely different from ourselves, we are displaying **vulnerability** about certain aspects of who we are while playing down others.

Which characteristics should we emphasize? Which should we play down? Using our past experience as a mirror, we can learn the answers. First, ask yourself which parts of your personality people tend to respond to best. The following list of adjectives can help you get started.

Outgoing	Technical	Risk-taking
Caring	Smart	Organized
Friendly	Warm	Spontaneous
Detailed	Productive	Stable
Creative	Cooperative	Positive
Action-oriented		

Just as you previously listed personality traits of your favorite sitcom star and talk-show host, you eventually will be able to fully list the traits of your own training persona. In evaluating the strengths of your personality, you'll discover a combination that's unique to you. Soon, you'll be a one-of-a-kind trainer—delivering content in an increasingly interesting, and consequently memorable, manner.

**Who are you as a trainer now? Use the space below
to describe your current "training character."**

_____

_____

_____

_____

_____

_____

IDENTIFICATION

-Linking Up with Your Participants-

During your process of **character development**, it's critical to keep in mind that whatever character finally evolves, it will be useless if the participants can't identify with it. Moviemakers know that there must be someone in the movie each viewer can identify with, or that movie won't involve all viewers emotionally.

Similarly, the best plays have a wide enough diversity of characters that almost everyone can identify with one of them. With which character do you identify most in Charles Dickens' classic play, *A Christmas Carol?* Are you Scrooge, Bob Cratchett, or Tiny Tim?

In our personal relationships, the people we feel closest to are usually those who have gone through life experiences similar to ours. As trainers, we must never lose sight of the fact that we are in a relationship with our participants. The more a group identifies with us, the closer the relationship will be.

Picture your favorite late-night talk-show host. With which trait(s) of his or hers do you identify most? Manner of speech? Style of dress? Interests? Hobbies? Sense of humor? Physical mannerisms? Write these common characteristics in the space below.

_____

_____

_____

_____

Have you noticed how talk-show hosts go to great lengths to avoid mentioning anything—like their hefty salaries or chauffeured limousines—that would cause their audience members not to identify with them? That could mean instant death for their careers!

At this point a good exercise might be to return to your "training character" description from the previous chapter and see if the traits you listed are ones with which your participants are likely to identify. Perhaps now's the time to list some of your weaknesses; no one can identify with perfection. What fears and struggles do you have that might cement the bond between you and your participants? Add them to your list in the previous chapter.

When your participants quickly identify with you,
the job of training is greatly simplified.

UNITY

-Making the Pieces Fit-

Try this multiphase experiment the next time you watch a late-night talk show.

Phase One

Watch the first half of the monologue with the volume turned down. Try to determine what the host is like by observing clothing, gestures, and other body language. Make a list of the qualities you perceive (e.g., introverted/extroverted, flashy/conservative, rich/poor, caring/unconcerned, comfortable/ill at ease, involved/aloof, sophisticated/down-home).

_____

_____

_____

_____

_____

_____

Phase Two

Now take your list in hand, turn up the volume, and turn your back to the screen. Listen to the host's voice for the remainder of the monologue. Do the voice, word choices, and/or content selection you hear conjure any additional personality qualities? Do they contradict any on your list?

Phase Three

Finally, watch the rest of the show with your revised list and see if the host says or does anything that contradicts the personality qualities you've listed. You undoubtedly will find significant consistency—or unity—among the host's clothing, mannerisms, walk, voice, and vocabulary. That unity has helped make that host a star!

On the other hand, have you ever heard DJs on the radio and then been shocked when you saw them in person? "They sure don't look like their voices!" you may have observed. Radio can tolerate considerable incongruence between a person's appearance and voice; television and live presentations cannot.

I once saw a magician who came onstage and performed a very sophisticated silent magic act, producing doves, cards, and coins to the strains of classical music. He wore a black tuxedo and really looked the part of the suave magician. Following his silent act, he reached into his pockets, began chatting, and started making balloon animals for the children present. You could feel the audience squirm as he began this portion of his act. I believe that the vast difference between this performer's sophisticated silent manipulations and his playful balloon tricks caused the audience to feel that one of these personae must be false. And once that thought enters an audience's mind, it affects the level of security and trust in the performer. As a result, the group doesn't let go and enjoy the performance as much.

For the sake of unity, that magician should consider having two different shows to feature his divergent performance styles. Or, by rethinking his character development, he should develop a performing character broad enough in personality to embrace both styles of performance.

To obtain and maintain participants' trust, we must present ourselves with unity in the following six areas.

Character
Which of your personality qualities do you want participants to see?

Costuming
Does your clothing selection match the description of your character?

Scripting
Do your word choices correspond to the description of your character?

Voice
Does your voice support the character traits you've chosen?

Motion
Do you move and gesture in keeping with the qualities you've chosen to project?

Content
Would someone with the character you're seeking to portray actually train in this content area?

Here's how this process looks in diagram form.

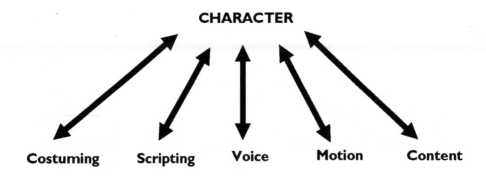

The five aspects of costuming, scripting, voice, motion, and content all support your training character, projecting your persona with a unified and consequently trustworthy image.

> How can you best judge your unity of presentation?
> Videotape yourself during a training session and
> conduct the talk-show-host experiment (from the
> beginning of this chapter)—with you as the subject.
> Any lack of unity quickly will become apparent!

THE PRESENTATION

THE TRAINER'S STAGE

-Positioning for Impact-

Imagine that you're in the audience at a Shakespeare play. "To be or not to be...," one actor says in a powerful voice. Look at the stage diagram below and picture the actor delivering his lines from each of the six areas. In your opinion, from which area would the actor deliver his lines with the greatest amount of force? The least?

A	B	C
D	E	F
Audience		

If you imagine the actor saying his lines from cell C and then from cell E, you can feel the amount of power cell E gives to a performer. Cell E (downstage/center) is the strongest of the cells for coming "into the face" of the audience. It's the stage position used most by solo performers.

Since it's the very nature of the television camera to turn any position into downstage/center, television isn't the best medium for judging the relative strength of stage positions. In a typical performance by a comedian, however, you'll notice that the upstage cells of A, B, and C are used very rarely, except for entrances and exits. In those rare cases, the comedian is likely walking through A, B, or C to get to E. In countries where reading is done from left to right, the strongest entrances are made from the audience's left and proceed to the right.

In order of strength, from most to least powerful, the cells are E, D, F, B, A, and C. We put objects we want to have "fade into the background" into cells A, B, and C; objects of emphasis appear in cells D, E, and F. What does all of this say to us as trainers? The following diagram illustrates how I use this knowledge in structuring the front "stage area" of my training room.

Participants

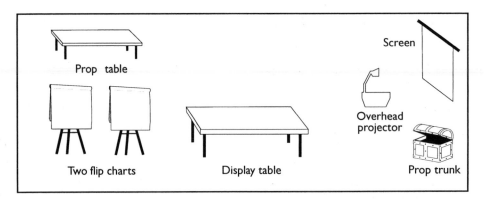

It was Bob Pike's *Creative Training Techniques Handbook* that introduced me to a similar arrangement. If I were right-handed instead of left-handed, I would switch the overhead projector, screen, and prop trunk with the flipcharts and **prop** table. Whenever possible, my training stage is at the end of the room opposite the entrance/exit door. I don't feel like competing for the training group's attention with people coming and going.

The display table holds materials I plan to use before the next break. The prop table holds materials I'll use later, in other sections of the day's training. The prop trunk is a locked trunk full of training props I use during the "request time" of the seminar. Because I'm a firm believer in trainers having a **"backstage** area" (which is off-limits to participants), there's only one easy way to get behind the display table—between that table and the overhead projector.

For 70 percent of my training, I present downstage center—*in front* of the display table. This positioning creates the greatest sense of **vulnerability**. Sometimes, I'll even bring a flipchart into that area to add impact to the visual. The impact of downstage/center is lost, however, if the trainer overuses the area and doesn't incorporate **variety** in his or her **motion**. I try not to stand in the downstage/center area when participants are working on a project. Then, by walking back into that area, I signal a beginning. Oftentimes, the contrast and change provided by your movement to another area will supply the needed emphasis to the point being made.

Diagram your own stage area. You'll be amazed at
what you learn!

BACKSTAGE

-Building One into the Training Room-

What makes going backstage at a show or a concert so special? Is it simply human nature—wanting what isn't readily available? Or the fact that not just anyone gets to go back there? Maybe we're hoping for a chance to talk to the actors (or musicians). Whatever the reason, scoring a backstage pass is a big deal for most of us.

If for no other reason than the universal curiosity about backstage areas, all trainers ought to have one. Every trainer needs an area that's off-limits to participants and solely under his or her control. Not to mention, a backstage area lends an important element of mystery to a training event!

But there are practical reasons, too. After all, why do shows and concerts have a backstage area? To put it bluntly, there's quite an array of unsightly stuff that goes into the making of a show—even a training show. There are boxes, bags, supplies, files, and materials for use later in the day. Leaving those mundane but necessary items out for everyone to see and access does little to foster a strong training atmosphere. Most support materials should be out of sight until they're brought forward during the process of **unveiling**.

Human nature ascribes greater value to **props** we aren't allowed to "paw through." As with the backstage issue, easy access destroys much of the mystery. In spite of this truth, I've seen trainers organize everything they were going to use for a seminar (including transparencies) on a participant-accessible display table. And I've watched participants rummage through those materials before the session even started. There were no surprises for those early attendees—no sense of **unpredictability**! These trainers relinquished their access to some very powerful showmanship tools because they lacked a backstage area for keeping materials out of sight until they were needed.

So, how can you keep participants away from your "training stuff" without alienating them? The following diagram of my training area shows how I work to maintain the privacy of my backstage area.

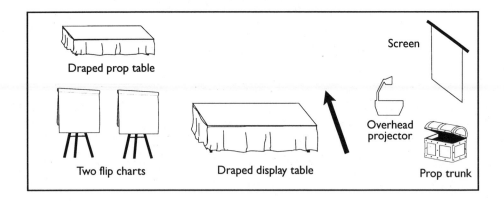

Draped prop table

Screen

Two flip charts

Draped display table

Overhead projector

Prop trunk

PARTICIPANTS

In most rooms, this arrangement affords me the most backstage space possible. The arrow indicates the only easy access to this area.

The draped tables provide me even more backstage space for storing boxes and other necessities (even my trash is often thrown under these). Only the items on the draped display table are easily accessible to participants, and I sometimes cover them with a sheet until I'm ready to use them.

Try it yourself...build a backstage area. You'll be
thrilled at the convenience it offers and by your
participants' fascination with it!

COLOR

-Using It Wisely-

Look at the colors you see on your favorite talk-show set. List all that you notice.

_____

_____

_____

_____

_____

_____

Why isn't there much bright red? Why not very much black?

What emotional reactions/images do the following colors stir in you?

Bright red_____ Light green _____

Burgundy_____ Bright green _____

Light blue _____ Dark green _____

Navy blue_____ Purple_____

Royal blue _____ White _____

Yellow_____ Black _____

Gold _____ Brown_____

Most people agree that brighter colors draw attention. The blues are relaxing. Purple, burgundy, royal blue, and gold are rich colors. Brown and black can be "heavy" colors and should be used sparingly for **contrast** or highlighting.

Now visualize the colors of the walls, carpeting, and ceiling in your training room and write them in the space below. What moods are generated by these colors? Are they the moods you want for your training?

_____

_____

_____

Take a moment to visualize the walls of a theater, particularly those adjoining the stage. What colors do you see? Most likely, you'll picture rich, dark colors—possibly gold and burgundy. Why don't we see more red-and-white striped walls in theaters? Because we don't go to theaters to look at the walls! The walls are colored not to bring attention to themselves but to create a mood that will help us focus on **the stage**.

A few years ago, this important aspect of the theater revealed itself to me in an unexpected way. I had a beautiful painting hanging in my home. In hopes of drawing people's attention to it, I purchased the most ornate frame I could find. But when people saw the painting, they commented only on the frame's intricate carvings, never once mentioning the painting itself! I then purchased a more conservative frame, and, as expected, most comments focused on the beauty of the painting.

What applications does this experience have regarding the colors we wear while training? Or the colors of our **props** and on our transparencies? One famous actor feels so strongly about the power of color that he'll never so much as appear in a scene with anything red—even a red purse! He knows that the brighter, more stimulating colors can distract from, and literally upstage, the performer, and he refuses to compete with a color!

Television provides constant reminders that colors can date us. Thanks to reruns, we'll never forget the rust carpeting and kitchen countertops in *The Brady Bunch*. **Currentness** requires that, as trainers, we keep our colors up-to-date.

I use bright colors for my transparencies, flipcharts, and props—anything seen only for a moment and then put away. The deeper, richer colors are saved for what I wear. The training room features more relaxing colors, with some earth tones added for depth and strength.

> What colors appear in your training room? What
> colors do you wear while training? Are these colors
> generating the mood you're trying to create?

SCENERY

-Generating Visual Support-

If I asked you to describe the background set of your favorite late-night talk show, could you do it? How detailed could you get? What **color** do you remember best?

In the space below, describe the set from memory, then watch the show and fill in any details you missed.

_____

_____

_____

_____

What does the set add to the show's success? How does it support the host? Do you find anything about it distracting?

Now, mentally transport yourself into a theater. You're watching the classic play, *A Christmas Carol*. It opens with a street scene outside the office of Ebenezer Scrooge. Storefronts and lampposts fill the stage. The first scene concludes, and the stage goes dim. Suddenly, you're in the office of Ebenezer Scrooge. There's Bob Cratchett sitting at his desk. Hey, wait a minute! The set from the first scene is still onstage—storefronts and all! The third scene takes you inside Bob Cratchett's house. But, as before, they've left the storefronts and the office scene and simply put the house set in front of the whole mess. This is getting ugly! "Lose the old scenery and props!" you want to stand up and yell.

Fortunately, you'll probably never have to sit through a theater production so devoid of good stage management. But why do so many trainers subject their participants to equally distracting scenery?

Let's take a brief detour here for a simple warning: Don't take the analogy of the training room being like a theater too far. The training room should *never* become a room in which participants passively watch a trainer perform. **Audience involvement** is mandatory if learning is to occur.

With that important point in mind, you'll want to ensure that when participants' attention is focused on the front of the room, the background maximizes **attention management**. If you're not conducting a seminar on how to quit smoking, move that big red No Smoking sign from the front of the room to a side wall, behind the peripheral vision of your participants.

During each break, put already-used visuals and props out of sight. If they won't be used again, put them away to make room for the new. For those that will be returned to, **unveiling** them again will infuse them with a newness that will enhance attention management.

Finally, consider for just a moment the phrase "change of scenery." Recently, I facilitated a two-day training in-house involving 30 trainers from a single company. We were into the afternoon session of the second day when I announced "request time," during which participants request a demonstration of any openers, closers, energizers, or review techniques from the *Tricks for Trainers* books. Although I'd accumulated quite a list of requests, I sensed the group's energy level dropping rapidly.

Upon my suggestion, we all stood up and left the training room for request time. After that change of scenery, the group returned refreshed for the remainder of the seminar. What could you teach outside your training room—or in any different surrounding—to maximize participants' retention by providing **variety** in your training-room scenery?

Take inventory of the scenery behind you when you train. At each break, change something about it. You'll feel the difference!

PRESTIGE

-Introducing the Trainer-

A world-renowned marriage therapist sat in a restaurant, unable to avoid hearing the conversation of the couple in the booth next to his. He knew that in their arguing, they were making a common communication error that he'd written about often in his dozens of best-selling books.

"Excuse me," he said to the couple. "I couldn't help overhearing your conversation." As he took a deep breath to share a piece of wisdom gained through more than 30 years as a therapist, they both turned to him and with one voice said, "Mind your own business!" Who could've guessed that within days, that same couple would be sitting in that same therapist's oak-paneled office, spending $120 an hour to hear the same advice that had been offered for free?

That's the power of an introduction! Without an appreciation for the messenger's prestige, we won't hear the most important message in the world.

Some evening, listen to a late-night talk show to hear how guests are introduced. What information does the host include in the introduction?

_____

_____

_____

What's omitted?

_____

_____

_____

What are your credentials for speaking on your training topic? List them below.

_____

_____

_____

_____

_____

_____

Most of us aren't fortunate enough to have someone announce our credentials before we start a training session. That shouldn't stop us from getting the appropriate information to our participants, though. Content retention demands it!

Why not place a printed introduction of yourself at each seat for participants to read prior to the session, or include it in your training manual? Following is a sample of the one I currently use.

DAVE ARCH

As a senior trainer for Bob Pike's Creative Training Techniques International, Inc., Dave Arch authored all three books in the Tricks for Trainers Resource Library (*Tricks for Trainers*, volumes 1 and 2, and *First Impressions/Lasting Impressions*) plus two videotapes and his newest books, *Showmanship forPresenters* and *Red Hot Handouts*.

In addition, Dave travels for Creative Training Techniques to more than 20 cities in the United States each year, presenting the Techniques and Tricks for Trainers seminar. For two days, he leads trainers through an experience of 119 attention-management techniques found in his books.

Dave has virtually pioneered the use of magic in training. Since 1982, magic has proven to be an effective communication tool for groups as diverse as hospital CEOs, sales representatives, and banking administrators.

Combining a 15-year background in personal and family counseling with a professional expertise in magic, Dave travels from his home in Omaha, Nebraska, to present his unique programs for some 25,000 people each year in both corporate and conference settings.

How would your introduction read? Use the credentials you listed earlier in this chapter to help you get started!

_____

_____

_____

_____

_____

_____

VULNERABILITY

-Revealing Yourself-

If you can easily identify personal qualities about your favorite performers, it's because those individuals have been vulnerable in revealing parts of themselves to you.

I believe we respond to vulnerability because of its key role in relationships. In the process of building an increasingly personal relationship, I share a part of who I am with you and you share a part of who you are with me. I share more and you share more as the relationship matures.

In a very real sense, the trainer is in a relationship—albeit a transient one—with participants. All of the rules that apply to the making of a successful personal relationship apply to the trainer/participant relationship. There must be trust, respect, honesty, and caring if the relationship is to satisfy both parties.

When I'm willing to be vulnerable with you, I express trust in you. I trust that you won't hurt me, that you won't take the material I'm sharing with you and use it against me. We love it when performers are willing to be vulnerable with us. And your participants love it when you express vulnerability with them!

When you're willing to share a part of yourself with them, you're giving participants something they want even more than your content. Your participants are infinitely more interested in you than in your material. As human beings, we're inherently more interested in people than in things.

The goal of the trainer, then, is to take that **intrinsic interest** inside all of us and build on it for effective content communication. One method of integrating our participants' interest in us with our content is by using personal illustrations and examples whenever possible. Instead of talking about how Henry Ford got someone to like him, talk about yourself. What challenges have you encountered trying to get someone to like you? How did you finally succeed?

But don't talk only about your successes; talk about your struggles, too. Sometimes the greatest points of **identification** with participants are based on our mutual struggles. How did you feel when you began doing what you now do so well? Use scenarios like this to build empathy and rapport with participants. Draw closer to the group by sharing common experiences of frustration and victory.

Getting back to our favorite performer, we can also learn a lot from what they *don't* share. They don't moan, groan, and complain about their personal problems. This would only drive their audiences away. Here's a simple rule for deciding what to share with participants: Make sure that the area of vulnerability you select is content-related. Ask yourself, "Does what I'm about to share enhance the content communication, or am I just getting something off my chest?"

One area of vulnerability that I've only recently begun exploring is that of asking a participant to do me a favor. Dale Carnegie suggested that one of the greatest ways to make a new friend is to ask that person for a favor. By doing so, we indicate that we trust that person to help us and we show vulnerability in expressing a need. When you need someone to help move a table, reposition the overhead, or assist with a demonstration, don't always ask the most outgoing participant. Experience has taught me that asking a more reluctant participant for a favor might win him or her over.

Finally, consider how to physically position yourself to appear as vulnerable as possible (see **Staging** for more ideas). Crossed arms, clenched fists, and a sideways (rather than full-front) stance all silently communicate a guarded posture. Try to avoid those positionings.

Have you ever wondered why leading performers don't stand behind podiums? Or why the most famous entertainers don't let anything bigger than a microphone get between themselves and their audiences? The greater the appearance of physical vulnerability, the greater the opportunity for mutual trust.

One of the primary benefits of incorporating vulnerability into your training is be the reduction of pressure on yourself. When you're vulnerable, you don't need to be The Great Provider of All Knowledge and Answers. What a relief!

When, during a training session, could you interject a personal illustration or revelation that would help your participants get to know you better? Write your ideas in the space provided below. Once you've made yourself vulnerable, you may just get hooked on its power!

_____

_____

_____

_____

PASSION

-Energizing Your Presentation-

If vulnerability is the beginning of self-revelation, passion is the power that moves it to the participants.

As you watch the opening monologue of a late-night talk show, observe the moments of passion in the host's communication with his or her audience and describe them in the space below.

_____

_____

_____

An author who's written a course for comedians on how to develop humor believes that one of the best ways to find new comedy material is to tape record a session in which you rant and rave about issues of significance to you—anything that really makes you *feel*. Then play the recording back and take notes. The author believes that a comedian's strongest material is always found in the arena of his or her passion. Sometimes the passion is anger, sometimes happiness, sometimes embarrassment. It always, however, involves the host releasing emotional energy in the direction of the audience. And audiences love it!

We love it because the expression of passion is a component of emotional **vulnerability**. We are truly going out on a limb when we express our feelings about a certain topic. We aren't sure how the group is going to respond, and our attitude says we don't care. We have something we feel so strongly about that we just have to express it.

In every training session you conduct, I hope you can identify some topic or idea about which you feel particularly passionate. Try to select at least one for each course you teach. Then, when you get to the designated place in the training content, give yourself permission to "go for it"!

No group ever leaves one of my seminars without understanding how much I abhor boring training sessions. Although some topics require a greater infusion of creativity, I firmly believe that with the resources available today, there's no excuse for a training session that puts participants to sleep.

So you see, I'm not necessarily talking about topics of a controversial nature. It might be something that everyone agrees on, but you are going to reveal the strength of your feelings to the group. Watch the difference it makes!

COSTUMING

-Communicating Character-

Try this experiment the next time you watch a late-night talk show. Turn down the volume for at least half the show. With no sound, you'll be able to focus on the host's clothing. Then, in the list below, check the traits that you feel apply to the host judging by his or her attire.

_____ Introverted

_____ Extroverted

_____ Wealthy

_____ Detail-oriented

_____ Stylish

_____ Aloof

_____ Pretentious

_____ Flashy

_____ Folksy

_____ Other: _____

Now repeat this experiment for several evenings to observe how much the host's attire varies. You'll probably observe a definite pattern to his or her clothing choices and be amazed at how much we can learn about a person's **personality** from the way s/he dresses!

Just as actors wear costumes to enhance the characters they play, talk-show hosts wear clothing that strengthens the personae they have decided to project. Their costuming serves as an extension of their **character development.**

In the following pairings, what do you think each item communicates about the personality of the person wearing it?

Suit	vs.	No suit
Double-breasted suit	vs.	Single-breasted suit
Long skirt	vs.	Midlength/short skirt
Skirt	vs.	Pants
Skirt and blouse/dress	vs.	Suit
Bright color/dark color	vs.	Earth tone
Sportcoat	vs.	Suit
Tie	vs.	Open shirt
Short-sleeve shirt	vs.	Long-sleeve shirt
White shirt	vs.	Colored shirt
Plain shirt	vs.	Patterned shirt

This chapter assumes you've already defined the character you wish to portray. If not, please turn to the **Character Development** chapter and complete the exercises there before continuing. If you've already defined your training persona, you're ready to turn to the **Character Development** chapter and re-read the description you wrote. Then, select attire that subtly supports and complements your training character.

> If participants could "turn down your volume" as you
> conduct training, what would your clothes alone
> reveal about you? Is that the image you want to
> project?

MOTION

-Moving with Purpose-

Magicians know that an audience watches what's moving. Consequently, they always move the hand they want the audience to watch while striving to keep stationery the hand they want the audience to ignore. And it works!

Trainers also use two types of motion: the motion that occurs while remaining in place and the motion that occurs when moving from one location to another.

Watch a talk show and pay special attention to when the host moves and, equally important, when s/he doesn't. Write your observations in the space below.

_____

_____

_____

You'll probably notice that talk-show hosts move when transitioning from one segment of the show to another (e.g., going from the monologue to guest interviews). They also may move closer to the camera when trying to intensify their control over the audience. Their hand gestures also serve to provide emphasis or direct attention.

When they want the focus on someone or something else, these individuals don't move. Watch them during an interview, and you'll notice that they almost freeze while the other person is talking— until they want the attention to return to themselves. If not overused, motion can be a powerful tool in **attention management**.

Trainers who habitually swing their arms, sway, or pace back and forth soon find themselves unable to access the powerful tool of motion. Like the boy who cried wolf, they have trouble getting and keeping the audience's attention; many of their motions fail to signal any noteworthy emphasis.

Try videotaping yourself while conducting a training session. It's the best way to make sure you're always moving with purpose!

HUMOR

-Laughing and Learning-

This chapter has already been written. You'll find its components through-out the book.

In the section titled **Mistakes**, you'll read about the three parts of every joke. The chapter titled **Passion** explains how to find comedy material by taping yourself while ranting and raving about a passionate topic. In the **Timing** chapter, you can experience the effect that a pause has on the delivery of a joke. It's in the chapter titled **Personality**, however, that you'll find the real se-cret to humor in the training room.

The best humor always comes from within. That's why the retelling of a joke often doesn't work; the "reteller" can't capture the personality of the person who told the joke in the first place. Truly great comedy occurs when just the right joke passes through just the right personality. And that's equally true of great singing, great magic, and great training.

I believe that every person can create laughter in others. Most of the time, however, we're not onstage. Instead, we're making a store clerk, a spouse, or an insignificant other laugh, so we don't pay attention. Consequently, we never learn what type of humor works best for us.

The next time a training group laughs at something you say or do, write it down. It's like being a humor detective—you'll soon discover clues that you can build on to solve this "case." Does your audience laugh at stories you tell about your kids? Your relationships? Your childhood? A definite pattern is likely to emerge.

And while we're on the subject of childhood, don't overlook yours as a source of great training stories. People love hearing about our early years; they know those years reveal a lot about us. Think about events in your childhood that support your content. Look for stories that happen to just about everyone. We laugh when **identification** occurs. Don't be afraid to tell stories about and on yourself. That type of humor strengthens your **vulnerability**.

Eventually, by combining your unique sense of humor with vulnerability and audience identification with passion, you'll produce a powerful combination that will bring you closer to your training group. And you'll have effectively il-lustrated your content, too— how efficient!

The next time you make someone laugh, try to determine why. Therein lies a clue for finding and refining your own style of humor.

CURRENTNESS

-Remaining Youthful-

When is a late-night talk-show host too old to do his or her job successfully? Although there's no magic age, there is a time: when he or she no longer seems youthful.

Now, I honestly don't believe that we're a youth-obsessed culture. Few of us actually crave the chance to relive our adolescence. Nevertheless, we're attracted to the qualities represented by youth. We're intrigued by youth's energy, enthusiasm for life, and interest in all things new and current—including the latest fashion trends and slang.

Youthfulness, as opposed to youth, has little to do with one's chronological age. Everywhere we look, we see old people in their 30s and young people in their 70s. It's not hard to spot those whose tastes are dated. Their clothing, decorating **color** choices, **intrinsic interests**, and vocabulary subliminally communicate that they no longer have the motivation to remain current.

Of course, I'm not advocating following every fad that comes along. Nor am I suggesting that, as trainers, we should act and talk like teenagers. But I do believe it's a very short leap from our participants' observations of our outdated speech or **costuming** to their assumption that we haven't kept up in the field in which we train. We then quickly lose valuable **prestige**, followed by a loss of participants' attention and, eventually, their trust.

What are your current interests? Do computers and their applications make the list? If not, it won't be long before you'll have trouble talking intelligently with your participants about an area very much on their minds.

Can you regularly contribute to conversations with your participants on topics that don't pertain directly to your content? If not, it may be an indication that staying current should become a priority for you.

> Let's agree to leave our bell-bottoms at home when
> training, no matter how much we once liked them.
> Let's move on!

MISTAKES

-Covering and Recovering-

Y ou may want to program your VCR for this exercise.

Record any late-night talk-show monologue. Chances are good that the audience will respond poorly to at least one joke in the routine. Pay particular attention to how the host recovers from the audience's rejection.

As you play back the tape, you'll notice that the delivery of the joke happened in three phases. The setup got the audience ready for the punch line: "Have you ever noticed how much a dog hates it when you blow in its face?" Then came the punch line: "Then why is it when you get the dog in the car, the first thing it does is hang its head out the window?" And the follow-through, or emotional tag, completed the sequence. In this scenario, the host might've shrugged in bewilderment; sometimes, comedians roll their eyes or sigh. Often, the follow-through is nonverbal.

Every joke and training exercise shares these three components. In a training exercise, the setup might be: "Let's talk at the tables about our most embarrassing moments on the job." The punch line usually comes when the table groups begin doing the exercise, and fresh **audience energy** is produced. The follow-through comes as the trainer reacts to the table groups beginning to do the exercise. At this point, it's not uncommon for trainers to hold their breath until all participants turn toward the others at their table and begin discussing the topic. Finally, there's a relieved exhale and a smile.

What if shortly into the exercise, however, your group is responding less than positively to the assignment? What should you do? What do the best performers in the business do when a bit doesn't "go over"?

Review your talk-show video to see how the host recovered from the less-than-enthusiastic response to a joke. You'll probably notice the host using the follow-through to get out of the predicament before quickly moving on. S/he might say something like, "These are the jokes, folks!" or "Testing...one, two, three—is this microphone on?" or, speaking to the cohost, "I told the writers that one wouldn't play!" But that's it—then it's time to move on. And don't believe for a second that those tag lines were ad-libbed. Every comedian develops a stock listing of such bailouts.

What lines could a trainer use to "recover" before moving on? The following have worked for me: "Well, *that* one didn't go anywhere, did it?" or, as you go over and write in your notebook, "Just reminding myself never to try *that* exercise again!" No audience wants to see a performer (or trainer) wallow in the distress caused by a failed joke (or training exercise). Few of us can stand to see a fellow human in pain.

Sometimes we're tempted to apologize or explain that "this has never happened before." Although this might make *you* feel better, it won't help your participants any.

Shrug it off and move on. Your participants will
respect you for it!

CLARITY

-Sending a Clear Message-

Have you ever heard a talk-show host tell a joke you didn't "get"? What do you think went wrong?

In all probability, one or both of two things happened. Either getting the joke required prior knowledge that you didn't have (e.g., the identity of the person who was the joke's focus), or the host didn't tell the joke clearly enough for you to understand it. It's hard to like a comedian whose jokes you don't get.

Likewise, it's hard to like a trainer whose content you don't get. Whenever our participants don't "get it," we've made the same mistake as the talk-show host described above. Either we assumed that they had prior knowledge that they didn't have, or we didn't present the material clearly enough.

Whether our content is simple or complex, clarity is essential—to both the entertainer *and* the trainer —and results from a three-stage process.

Just as performers must know their audience, we must first *know our participants*. We can't assume that they know what we know. We can't assume what they know or don't know. (This is where I most often get into trouble.)

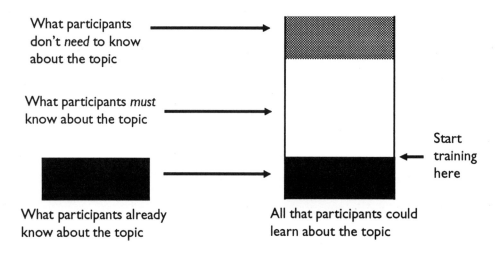

What participants don't *need* to know about the topic

What participants *must* know about the topic

Start training here

What participants already know about the topic

All that participants could learn about the topic

Second, we must pare down our content and *eliminate all nonessentials*. With no mercy, we must answer the question, "What must participants know to be successful in the area in which we're training? The longer we've been training in an area of content, the harder answering this question becomes. That's because the more we know about any area, the more difficult it is to pinpoint exactly what is essential about that which we know. If the preceding question is answered with complete honesty, some truly good material will need to be cut from your course. However, this material can always be put into print (see **Printed Programs**), making it available to those who want to learn more than the mere essentials.

Finally, we must organize the remaining content so that we *begin where the participants' knowledge leaves off* and take participants, step by step, where we want them to be.

Knowing participants, eliminating nonessentials, and starting training where participants' knowledge leaves off will give any training session a pinpoint focus that will definitely increase its impact.

Applying this three-stage process to your content
will help your participants "get it"!

ROUTINING

-Plotting Your Course-

I view training as an art—specifically, a narrative art form. The organization of a training session is much like the carefully crafted plot of a good book or the routining of a well-scripted movie, play, or show.

What is the overall routine of a late-night talk show? Isn't there a high degree of sameness and **predictability** from one to the next? Virtually every one features:

- The warm-up

- The introduction

- The monologue

- Banter

- Talking guest(s)

- Musical guest(s)

- The closing

It's as though the producers of these shows have found a magic formula. As long as the public keeps watching, it must be working!

So, what happens during each of the seven talk-show segments, and what can we as trainers learn from each?

The warm-up occurs outside the eye of the television audience. A guest comedian and/or the host comes out and works with the studio audience before the television cameras start rolling. The **warm-up** is designed primarily to unite the individual members of the audience as a group and then create a team spirit between the host and the audience.

In training, the warm-up is the time when the trainer meets and talks with participants before the session officially begins. S/he may even present a brain-teaser activity for small-group interaction prior to starting the class.

The introduction frames the host, bestowing the **prestige** s/he deserves. This helps build expectations in relation to the show's content and exhibits respect for the one who will manage the show. There is also the initial **unveiling** of the show's agenda through the listing of guests and special features.

In lieu of a formal introduction for a trainer, his or her credentials might simply be printed and placed on each table or with the class materials. To ensure maximum receptivity to the content, the trainer's credentials must be communicated in some manner prior to training. Pretraining **publicity** helps build anticipation and foster realistic expectations among participants.

The monologue is the official **opening** of the show and serves to link the television audience, the studio audience, and the host. It gives the host a chance to communicate his or her **personality**, express **vulnerability** and **passion**, and bond with the audience through **identification**. This is also the segment during which the host first shares the program agenda with the audience.

In the training room, this is the opening of the training session. It gives the trainer a chance to self-express as well as to shift the participants' mental focus from where it is to where it needs to be for maximum content retention.

The *banter* segment of talk shows takes the ingredients of the monologue and extends them to other members of the staff and/or audience. Sometimes, **audience participation** activities, which physically involve audience members, happen during this segment. Sometimes, it's simply the host bantering with the cohost.

The trainer might have participants create their own name cards or participate in a similar icebreaker during this section of training. Physical audience involvement is crucial during this phase to ensure that all learning styles have been encouraged to actively participate in the learning process.

The *talking guest(s)* segment most closely corresponds to the content-presentation section of a training class. The talk-show host has chosen the interview technique to communicate that content. After ensuring the audience members are comfortable with each other (the warm-up) and with him or her (the monologue and bantering), the host is ready to move into a section with less direct audience involvement. Guests are invited onstage to participate in interviews with the host. On average, this segment doesn't occur until nearly 40 to 50 percent of the show is over. Relational activities between the host and the audience often take up to 50 percent of the show's allotted time!

The trainer is now ready to communicate content using a wide variety of methods. Unlike the talk-show host, the trainer isn't limited to the interview technique.

The *musical guest(s)* segment supplies **variety** and **contrast**, providing the audience with an opportunity to take a relaxing mental break before the closing. Involving the least audience involvement, the musical segment usually lasts five minutes or less.

During training, adequate mental and physical breaks not only help replenish audience energy but also give the trainer a chance to regroup.

The closing gives the host a chance to achieve closure while enticing the audience with the schedule of the next evening's show. The music is usually celebratory in nature.

As the training session draws to a close, "bringing down the curtain" with a sense of finality ensures a sense of satisfaction and fulfillment for both the trainer and the participants.

Although such a structure allows for considerable **unpredictability** and **planned spontaneity**, it's obvious that much thought has gone into its arrangement.

> May we be as thoughtful in organizing our training
> sessions. The next chapters—focusing on
> **progression, flow, variety, contrast,** and
> **tempo**—will give us the tools to do just that!

PROGRESSION

-Moving Forward-

"This isn't going anywhere!" I've made that comment many times while reading books or watching television. It's been heard to leave my lips while in an audience at a play or a movie. I've even been known to say it while listening to music. And it always indicates the lack of one vital ingredient in the art form at hand: *progression*.

Progression gives the audience a feeling that the program is moving forward. If the feeling of progression ebbs at any juncture, the audience may develop the sense that it's standing still or wandering in purposeless circles.

Naturally, such a feeling is discouraging. If you're watching a television program, you're likely to turn it off. When a sense of progression is absent in the training room, participants turn *us* off! But if you listen carefully to either the initial introduction of any late-night talk show or to the host at the end of the monologue, you'll discover the first of four secrets for developing a sense of progression. By listing the guests and other features, the announcer and the host both *present the audience with an agenda*. What do you hear communicated about the program in those few fateful moments? Write your response below.

As discussed in the **Publicity** chapter, expectations are set not only in terms of guests and special features but also in relation to the overall tone of the show. "You're going to have good time during this program!" is the unspoken communication from a late-night host to the audience.

The announcement of the agenda is actually the process of setting goals for both the audience and the host. The host declares what s/he plans to accomplish with the audience's involvement over the next 60 minutes. When the goals have been accomplished, the program will be over. The audience and the host will have successfully completed what they set out to do. There will have been progression, and there will be a sense of satisfaction in its completion.

As you continue to watch, notice how often the host *repeats the show's agenda.* Usually, the remaining components of the agenda are reiterated before each commercial break. This second secret adds to the sense of progression. It's as though the host is announcing, "Congratulations! Some of our goals have been accomplished, and here's what remains." Checking back to the agenda at various stages of completion adds to the sense of progression.

Now, imagine an unplanned, unannounced guest suddenly appearing on the program and talking about the terrible plight of the world's homeless. The guest wasn't announced, and her presentation hardly fits the promised tone of the show. Of course, this happens almost annually during the presentation of the movie Oscars. The event kicks off with a certain glamour, a scripted agenda, and an overall **unity** of tone. Then, some award presenters and recipients use their moments in front of the camera to plug their personal causes. Often, they just don't fit.

Therein lies the third secret to creating the feeling of progression during training: *maintain unity.* Once the agenda is set, we must ensure that each component relates to that agenda and helps accomplish the overall goals established there.

Then, when the agenda has been completed, we put the fourth and final secret into play: *move into the **closing***. There's nothing more frustrating to a group than an agenda that keeps lengthening into what feels like an eternity!

Using a travel analogy, I propose that a sense of progression occurs during training when we:

> Tell participants where we're going; inform them of upcoming landmarks, stay on the most direct route; and stop when we've arrived!

FLOW

-Smoothing Out the Presentation-

I do enjoy watching ice-skating. The beauty of the skaters and the reactions of the crowd are wonderful. I equally enjoy listening to great singing. The singer begins a song and smoothly sings it to the end. Again, you have a performer interacting with an audience.

Listen to the audience, however, when a skater falls. There's a collective gasp as the audience members draw in their breath in unison. It's like no other sound in the world. Or listen to the crowd when a singer forgets the words to a song. A pained silence takes control. As audience members—as human beings—we enjoy smoothness and recoil at the first sign of jerkiness.

To give training the smoothness of an accomplished ice-skater, attention must be paid to both the logical flow and the physical flow of the training session.

Most content has a sequential pattern to it—there's a beginning, a middle, and an end. By determining that logical progression, or *logical flow*, you'll smooth out training by eliminating unnecessary backtracking and jumping ahead.

There are also physical considerations in relation to flow. Say, for example, you're preparing for an activity that requires rearranging your room's tables and chairs. This would be a great time to think of another activity involving the tables and chairs in the new configuration. Here, you're considering the *physical flow* of the training session.

Adequate **rehearsal** greatly improves a session's physical flow. Pity the participants who have to sit through a session where the trainer is forever asking, "Now, where did I put that?" while digging around for an overhead transparency, a **prop**, or a workbook page. There can be no flow in such a scenario. The training session only jerks along to a merciful end.

Let's look again at the ingredients listed in the **Routining** chapter to see how flow affects the smoothness of a late-night talk show.

- The warm-up

- The introduction

- The monologue

- Banter

- Talking guest(s)

- Musical guest(s)

- The closing

Now imagine for a moment a talk show beginning with a guest interview, then moving into part of the monologue, then going to another guest interview, then returning to the monologue. Something would feel terribly wrong!

Fortunately, you'll never have to endure such a show.
Your training participants shouldn't have to, either!

VARIETY

-Banishing Boredom-

Reflect for a moment on a late-night talk show. Describe all of the ways you can think of in which variety is introduced into a rather rigid format. Here's my list.

Location. The **scenery** changes. Sometimes the host is inside the studio, sometimes outside. Sometimes the host is onstage, sometimes in the audience.

Music. Moods are created and dismantled as various styles, tempos, and volumes of **music** are interspersed throughout the show.

Special features. These include the monologue, skits, **props, audience involvement,** film clips, **giveaways**, dialogues, demonstrations, and guest interviews.

Lighting. Sometimes the lighting is full bright, sometimes subdued. Sometimes it's colored, sometimes pure white.

Tempo. Whether the speed of delivery is fast or slow, the **tempo** fits the content and typically sits in **contrast** to other segments of the show.

Trainers have all of these components—and
more—at their disposal, too. How many do you use
in your training?

CONTRAST

-Emphasizing the Importance-

We love contrast! It's the beauty of winter changing into spring into summer and then into fall. If you listen to the song arrangements on a CD, you'll quickly recognize the pattern of a slow song followed by a fast song, a quiet song followed by a louder song.

Contrast is important for maintaining both participants' interest and their involvement. Content presentation featuring too much of the same—a lack of variety—loses its capacity to captivate participants' attention. A trainer can use concrete as well as abstract contrast to aid content communication.

Concrete contrast concerns itself with an actual physical object in relation to its immediate surroundings. As explained in the section on **attention management**, any object that contrasts with its surroundings in size, color, or shape will immediately become a focus of participants' attention. Trainers can use this fact to their advantage in organizing the room and its **scenery** as well as in displaying **props**. When I turn on the overhead and project it onto a screen in a dark corner, I'm using concrete contrast. When I place a stark white piece of paper against a dark background, I'm using concrete contrast. When I use a **prop** that's either very small or very large, I'm using concrete contrast.

Abstract contrast in the training room involves such inanimate and subtle considerations as the tempo of specific training sections and the volume and pitch of sounds. On the first day of the Techniques and Tricks for Trainers seminar, training moves at quite a rapid **tempo**. Then, in the middle of the afternoon, I distribute copies of *Tricks for Trainers, Volume 1,* and each person quietly scans a section of the book in anticipation of presenting a short review of that section to the participants at his or her table. Classical **music** plays in the background, and the contrast of this section's tempo with the rest of the seminar is dramatic. This slower tempo is so enjoyable for participants that I've allotted up to 45 minutes for this activ y. Participants embrace the contrast!

As you build your training **routine**, consider using
contrast for maximum impact!

TEMPO

-Feeling the Speed-

Tempo—the actual speed at which a trainer delivers content. This chapter stands in contrast to the **Pacing** section, in which we focus on participants' subjective sense of the speed at which time passes in the training room.

Watch a talk-show host move through the various program segments and notice when things speed up and when they slow down. Listen particularly to the speed of the guest interviews. Why these changes in tempo?

When the audience members provide little or no positive feedback to an interview, watch how quickly the host terminates it and moves on to something more interesting for the audience. Notice also how the host slows down and "milks" the interviews that provoke strong **involvement** and **audience response**.

Wise trainers also vary their speed of delivery. Here are three reasons for doing so.

The *level of audience involvement* is the first. As noted in the **Mistakes** chapter, when something isn't working, move on as quickly as possible. When something *is* working, slow down to maximize impact and retention.

Contrast is the second reason to vary content-delivery speed. If you attend an hour-long concert, you'll want to hear some fast-paced selections (to keep you awake and energized) and some slow numbers (to give you a break and time to relax). Training participants need the same variety. Notice how the segments of a late-night talk show contrast with each other. See the **Contrast** chapter for a more detailed examination of this important training component.

The *personality of the group* is the third consideration in varying the speed of delivery. Some groups require a quicker presentation than others. New trainers find out quickly that training groups, just like individuals, have distinctive personalities. When the overall personality of a group might be described as decisive, with a "cut to the chase" orientation, the wise trainer delivers rapidly. When the group is characterized by a steadiness and overall cautious approach, a slower delivery usually matches the mood of the room more closely.

Trainers who don't give tempo much consideration typically deliver content at the speed most comfortable for them. But remember:

All content can be presented at a variety of speeds.
And trainer flexibility concerning delivery speed
always increases training effectiveness.

CONFLICT/RESOLUTION

-Dramatizing Content-

If you've ever started reading a book or watching a movie late at night and found yourself unable to stop and go to bed at a reasonable hour, you know firsthand the power of the common narrative technique explained in this chapter. First there's the conflict, then there's the curiosity about the resolution. Think for a moment how much of our lives is spent caught up in the power of the conflict-resolution cycle. It engages us when we watch the news, read the newspaper, watch a sitcom or game show, or attend the circus.

Haven't we all leaned forward in our seats as the trapeze artist misses the triple somersault and bounces into the net below? Second try, same fate. Finally, on the third attempt, the performer successfully completes the maneuver—to the exuberant applause of the audience. In all probability, that applause would have been a mere shadow of itself had the performer accomplished the feat the first time around. The failed attempts heightened the conflict and made its resolution all the more satisfying.

Hidden from the audience by a screen, master showman and escape artist Harry Houdini often escaped from his restraints a full 15 to 20 minutes before coming out from behind the screen. It's said that he once sat backstage reading the newspaper until a stagehand informed him that the rustling of the pages could be heard in the audience. (Houdini responded that the band should play louder.) Like the trapeze artist, Houdini knew the power of building suspense through protracting the time between the conflict and its resolution.

In the stage play *Frankenstein*, the monster ominously threatens to return on his creator's wedding night. The audience anticipates that return. In a final scene, the bride is getting dressed for her wedding and moves toward a large wardrobe closet to get her veil. You can feel the audience tense up. An interruption prevents her from opening the closet door—not once, but three times.

With each interruption, the suspense builds. The audience becomes convinced that the monster lurks inside the wardrobe. Finally, the bride opens the door and...."Make them care and then make them wait" is how Darwin Ortiz describes this important element of drama in his book, *Strong Magic*. In *Frankenstein*, the playwright first made us care about the bride, Elizabeth. If we didn't care about her, we wouldn't mind if the monster jumped out of the closet.

As trainers, we must begin by helping our participants care about us. We can do this by sharing our personality with them through identification and vulnerability. We are then in a much better position to make them care about our content.

The trainer can focus conflict in at least two directions in the training room.

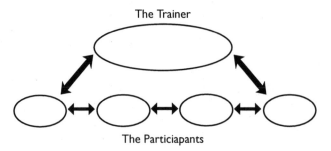

Conflict with the trainer quite often involves curiosity about the trainer and/or the content. What's s/he going to do next? What's s/he really like? Why is that prop sitting in the front of the room? By making participants care (become curious) and sustaining that tension until the communication of content occurs, we tap into a powerful training formula. By giving anticipation inadequate time to do its work, we rob the resolution of its power to impact.

At the end of the two-day seminar titled Techniques and Tricks for Trainers, we have a closing ceremony that features what we call "The Lighting of the Pickle." The room lights are dimmed, and a dill pickle is plugged into the wall and lights up like a fluorescent lightbulb! The activity is used to illustrate a summarizing emphasis and to bring closure to the seminar. However, The Lighting of the Pickle is mentioned at the end of the first day, then throughout the second day. Consequently, when it finally occurs, it receives the attention it deserves.

Conflict with other participants can involve competition. Who's going to win? What are they going to win? How are they going to win? Realizing the training power of competition, Creative Training Techniques wisely offers a two-day seminar that examines nothing but the creative use of games and graphics in the training room. Wouldn't it be great to harness this captivating technique of drama and employ it to increase participants' content retention?

May each of our training sessions unfold like a well-written novel. That's what I'm shooting for!

PLANNED SPONTANEITY

-Breathing Life into the Room-

You've seen it countless times...a late-night talk-show host is sitting behind the desk and suddenly appears to receive an inspiration. After an exchange with the show's director, the host offers up a suggestion—something like, "Hey...why don't we go outside and see what's happening?"—and immediately, an entire camera crew hits the street! True spontaneity? Hardly. But certainly spontaneous-*appearing*...and we love it!

Why do people enjoy spontaneity? Why does even *planned* spontaneity bring energy into a room? I'm convinced that the principle behind this technique has been experienced by every trainer who's ever dropped something, stumbled, or had the overhead bulb burn out. When such unexpected things happen, participants are energized, look up, and pay attention. Are they maliciously lying in wait for us to mess up? I don't think so.

At the heart of the issue is the fact that participants are far more interested in who we are than in our content. This is a logical extension of my belief that people are infinitely more interested in other people than in things.

When all goes well and I'm smoothly moving through my content, my training class may get a chance to know my material but usually doesn't get a chance to know me. When I stumble, drop something, or have a bulb unexpectedly expire, though, my participants know they'll have a chance to see more of the real me. What will I say? What will I do? How will I react? Inquiring minds want to know.

If this type of experience, common to nearly every trainer, gives us a glimpse into the power of the spontaneous, the next question is: How can we use that power in our seminars even when things go according to plan? By planning spontaneous-appearing events, we can tap that power when we need it—anytime!

In the two-day seminar I facilitate, a simple magic trick is taught to illustrate teamwork. Two pieces of yarn join together right in front of the participants' eyes. Based on the principle of planned spontaneity, I suggest that any trainer using this illustration would go into the room before the training group arrived and toss the yarn on the floor. Later, when it came time to do the trick, the trainer pretended to see the yarn out of the corner of his eye. Acting as though he'd been hit with a sudden inspiration, he picked it up and went into the illustration.

That trainer increased the effectiveness of the illustration 100 percent. By giving it the feeling of spontaneity, he gave it the feeling of life itself...after all, life is very spontaneous! Certainly, the trainer could've removed the yarn from the training table, a briefcase, or a pocket, but it wouldn't have carried nearly the power that it did when framed as a spontaneous-appearing event.

Whenever you're using a common prop to make a point, act as though you suddenly found it in the training room. Whenever possible, tie your upcoming content to a spontaneous comment made by one of your participants. Although you've told a story many times before, act as though it just hit you as a good illustration of the point you're making.

You'll notice the difference.
And so will your participants!

UNPREDICTABILITY

-Using Surprise for Impact-

When I was taking college classes, I spent a good deal of time doodling on pieces of paper while professors lectured. One of my doodles looked like this:

It was my visual depiction of boredom. Labeled, the lines looked like this:

SPEAKER

LISTENER

The listener hears the nature of the topic and anticipates what the speaker is going to say, and the speaker says exactly what the listener predicted—two parallel lines pointing toward eternal boredom.

From time to time, I heard interesting speakers and diagrammed their presentations like this:

SPEAKER

LISTENER

Here, the listener tries to anticipate where the speaker is going (as we all do). The speaker, however, takes a turn that the listener didn't anticipate. This change-up is the heart of every great joke.

Do you remember when you first heard the joke, "What's black and white and red all over?" You thought and thought. When the answer "a newspaper" came, you realized that the homonyms "red" and "read" had tricked you, and you laughed your heartiest first-grade laugh!

The second time you heard the joke, you didn't laugh; it had become predictable. The "speaker" and "listener" lines once again had become parallel. Only when the new punch line—"a sunburned zebra"—started making the rounds did you laugh at the joke again. Such twists are what keep comedy writers in business.

To watch Bob Pike use his Trainer Bingo in a large group of unsuspecting trainers is indeed a lesson in the power of unpredictability. Each person receives a bingo card and begins to play what appears to be a regular game of bingo. Bob calls the numbers, and the players cross off different ones on different cards. However, the specially designed cards make it possible for Bob to call one number that will make the entire room jump up and yell "Bingo!" at the same time. And when they do, the energy of unpredictability needs no further discussion.

We pay millions of dollars to have skilled performers treat us to unpredictability in movies, plays, and comedy monologues around the nation. Let's use this powerful force in our training rooms, too!

Answer the following questions to check your understanding of participants' training expectations.

1. How do your participants expect you to open the training session?

_____

2. When do they expect you to announce breaks?

_____

3. How do they expect the room to be arranged for training?

_____

4. How do they expect you, as their trainer, to dress?

_____

5. Do they expect you to serve break refreshments? If so, what?

_____

6. What audiovisual aids do they expect you to use?

_____

7. How do they expect you to close the training session?

_____

8. What could you do differently in any of the preceding areas to create an energized atmosphere of unpredictability?

_____

_____

_____

_____

Unpredictability, successfully used, generates disequilibration among participants—and that's good! By keeping the group "off balance"—never knowing what's coming next—you help maintain teachability in the classroom. **Predictability** breeds unteachability.

Watch the late-night talk shows to understand the concept of balance, and see how each has found just the right amount of unpredictability. Each show has found a formula that works in light of its host's personality and strengths. The show's producers follow that format formula every night of the week.

Within that **routining**, however, they also have ample room for unpredictability with every show.

And so do you!

PREDICTABILITY

-Initiating Your Own Training Traditions-

What do you know is going to happen on your favorite talk show every night?

_____

_____

_____

_____

You probably responded that the show will open with a monologue by the host, and you'd be disappointed if it didn't. Then, there will be banter with the bandleader, and you'd be disappointed if there weren't. Why do you like knowing such things about the show? Because there's something to be said for traditions.

My family hosts an annual Easter brunch. Each person brings something, and we share in the meal together. It's a tradition, and we enjoy the feelings that traditions create. They bring us security through stability.

Usually, the late-night talk show's traditions revolve around **routining**. There's a typical routine followed each and every evening. Within the context of that routine, however, an infinite number of variations exists. **Variety** and **unpredictability** are never sacrificed for the sake of predictability.

Seasoned trainers have developed a formula not unlike the talk-show routine. They have tested it and proven that it works, no matter what the content. Participants who train with such facilitators benefit from a pattern that offers stability in the midst of changing content and class-specific components.

My own training has evolved into a pattern consisting of a physically involving group activity quickly followed by an opportunity for participants to share about themselves with others at their table. I then deliver a brief monologue during which I share in a manner that bridges to the content at hand (see **Opening** and **Vulnerability**). This formula has worked well for me. Although activities change from class to class, and the content of my opening monologue varies, the pattern has become a familiar tradition to those who attend my training. It brings stability to those "iffy" opening moments of the training experience.

What do your participants know is going to happen during every one of your sessions?

_____

_____

_____

_____

Why do they like those traditions? What new
traditions might you like to add?

MUSIC

-Communicating the Mood-

The use of music on talk shows is barely noticeable to most people. If you listen for it, however, you'll soon discover that it's indispensable.

Besides featuring guest bands or singers, how do talk shows use music? When do they use it? What types of music do they use? What would be different if they didn't use it? With those four questions, a strategy for the use of music in training slowly evolves.

Talk shows use music at the beginning and end of the show—in most cases, it's their theme song. It's usually the most upbeat, powerful music of the show. Not quite as obvious, however, is their use of music when they go to and come back from commercials (trainers call them breaks). This music is usually not as powerful as the opening and closing theme and often reflects the nature of the content just discussed. In other words, sober content is not generally exited with a polka.

You'll also find these shows using music to fill "dead spaces." For instance, when the host walks from center stage to the desk, the tune played is designed to sustain the **audience energy** generated during the monologue.

What moods or scenes do the following types of music bring to mind for you?

Classical _____   Country _____

Rock _____   Heavy metal _____

Pop _____   Novelty tunes _____

Jazz _____

Each musical style conveys its own set of images. Without saying a word, you influence your participants' expectations of training with the type of music you select.

Bob Pike has done a marvelous job with a difficult assignment in selecting a variety of training music for both volumes of his *Powerful Presentation Music* cassettes for trainers. Each volume contains three audiocassettes. One cassette contains the broader, higher-energy music that's perfect for **opening** and

closing. The second cassette contains classical-type music to serve as background for discussions, while the third cassette contains novelty tunes (goofy music) that are perfect for breaks and games. Wisely, Bob has stayed away from musical extremes that can prove controversial and typically don't wear as well as the middle-of-the-road stylings.

When conducting daylong training, I prefer to use the higher-energy music in the morning, with a shift toward the novelty tunes in the afternoon. Interspersed throughout are the classical-sounding selections that gently fill the energy void when groups are involved in discussions or personal planning.

The wise use of music in your training will have your participants singing a different tune!

UNVEILING

-Lifting the Curtain-

The sculptor has completed a new piece of work, and it's about to be unveiled. A hush falls over the crowd as the covering is removed. People gasp as they see the piece of art for the first time. We love the removal of coverings...we love unveilings!

What does an unveiling silently communicate? Doesn't it tell us we're about to see something valuable and out of the ordinary? After all, we don't throw a covering over our kitchen table and unveil it before every meal.

I'm convinced that when someone comes through a curtain from **backstage** to begin a performance, that individual is actually being unveiled—much like that sculpture—with all of the importance associated with any unveiling. Could a talk-show host just be sitting in the audience at the beginning of the show, then walk from the audience to the stage? Of course. Would we like it as much? Not a chance!

What can you unveil during your training process? Here are some ideas.

Unveil your materials. Rather than distributing your printed workbook materials as participants enter the room or having them in lace at the table, turn the distribution of the materials into a ceremony. Bring the materials forward and ceremoniously present them to participants, handing out only the materials needed for that particular part of the class. You may even want to try covering your materials with a bedsheet or large tablecloth until you're ready to distribute them. Treat your printed materials as valuables, and you'll be amazed at how quickly the group picks up on your attitude.

Unveil your content. Rather than creating a workbook so complete that anyone could learn your content simply by reading the book, produce one that includes blanks participants need to fill in during class. Likewise, leave entire pages in outline form, and participants can supply the fine points.

Unveil your transparencies. Don't flash an entire transparency on the screen at once. When appropriate, use a piece of paper to cover some information, then ceremoniously move the covering to reveal more and more of your points.

*Unveil your **props**.* Every time a training group returns from a break, something should be different in the front of the room (**The Trainer's Stage**).

Some materials should be put away (because you're done with them) and some new items should be displayed (because you're about to use them). Many trainers make the mistake of setting everything out at the beginning of the session and waiting until the end to put everything away. Silently, that communicates to participants that there really isn't anything very special about any of it.

Unveil your flipcharts. Don't display an important flipchart sheet before you're ready to use it. Instead, prepare it ahead of time and turn it over the back of the flipchart. Then you can dramatically flip it over to the front when you're ready for all to see it.

Unveil your room. Whenever there's room for early arrivers to congregate outside your room, open the doors no more than 30 minutes before training begins. When people sit in a room for 45 minutes or longer, principles of **attention management** tell us that the room is no longer fresh for them. Your participants are curious to see the room, so build their anticipation and keep the room "fresh" longer by waiting to open it.

The next time you train, try an unveiling. You'll immediately feel its power!

SCRIPTING

-Putting It into Words-

Every trainer I've ever known eventually worked from a script. Usually, these scripts aren't put into writing. They evolve, however, when trainers teach the same material over and over again. The reason for this is easy to understand. The very nature of language implies that there is a better way, and consequently a worse way, to say what we want to say. For trainers, clarity, character, and class involvement lead us to the better way.

Clarity. This factor is most apparent in the giving and receiving of directions. When blank stares greet our explanations, we modify. Clarity demands that we refine what we say until we're able to communicate our content as clearly as possible. As we saw in the **Clarity** chapter, the process involves paring away all nonessential material, then meeting participants where they are.

Character. There are countless ways to say any given thing. The decisions made after reading the **Character Development** section determine how we'll choose to express ourselves. If I'm introducing a section in which I'm about to express my **passion** on a given subject, I might say any of the following:

- "With your permission, let me express my feelings on this matter," or

- "I feel a pontification coming on," or

- "I'm getting ready to step up on my soapbox!" or

- "Be warned! I'm about to let it all hang out!"

Take a moment to visualize the type of trainer who would use each of these introductory statements. How would that person be dressed? What type of personality would s/he have? Which of the statements comes closest to the way you'd say it?

Listen to the word choices of several late-night talk-show hosts. Compare one host to another. What do their word choices tell you about their personalities? Education levels? If our word selection doesn't match our training persona, unity is disrupted and participant trust is undermined.

Class involvement. When **audience participation** is the goal of the session, there are several approaches we can take to scripting that will increase the desired participant involvement. First, we must be sure we're speaking to the education/sophistication level of our audience. Consider the talk-show hosts you just compared and try to determine the grade level at which each typically speaks. At what grade level do you speak to your participants? Our participants' involvement with our content requires that we speak neither beneath them nor over their heads. Often, this requires the trainer to have several different presentations for the same content.

In addition to the education-level factor, the experienced trainer understands that there are specific ways to dramatically involve participants in what you have to say. As an opening to the two-day Techniques and Tricks for Trainers seminar, I relate the story of a state fair pitchman I saw during my childhood. This story can be told at least three different ways. The least effective Noninvolved Listener Approach begins, "There once was a man at the state fair who...." The more effective and more personal Passive Observer Approach begins, "I once saw a man at the state fair who...." At least here, the trainer is about to express **vulnerability** through self-revelation. The most effective Active Participant Approach begins, "Come with me to the state fair. Look, there's a man over there who...." Careful attention to scripting allows the final level to draw participants into the story as actively involved participants.

> When clarity, character, and class involvement
> dictate how we say what we want to say,
> participants' content retention increases!

TIMING

-Pausing for Punch-

An old-time entertainer, attempting to advise a young novice, started out, "Do you know what I believe to be the most...." "Timing!" the novice aggressively interrupted. Obviously, the novice understood the word but not the concept.

Timing, as defined in this book, is the amount of space between two events, two spoken phrases, or a spoken phrase and an event. The next time you watch the monologue on a late-night talk show, notice the time intervals between the host's setup of a joke, the punch line, and the follow-through. What if the host had flailing arms throughout the joke? What if s/he had left a longer interval between the joke's setup and its punch line? A shorter interval? How would these variations have affected the audience's response?

Try the following experiment with friends or family members. Pose the question, "What did the duck say when it bought a tube of lip balm at the drugstore?" Follow up with the punch line, "Put it on my bill!" First, tell the joke with no pause between the question and the punch line—don't even breathe between the two. Then try it again, counting to 10 between the question and the punch line. Finally, tell the joke one last time, counting to three between the question and the punch line.

Can you feel the difference? When there's no breath between the two components, the response from your audience members will be minimal. You haven't given them time to process the question before moving on to the punch line. When you count to 10 between the two components, the audience will stop caring by the time you deliver the punch line. The longer you make an audience wait for the punch line (or any resolution in the **conflict/resolution** formula), the stronger it must be. When you count to three between the setup and the punch line, you've found just about the right pause. The audience has time to process the question and still cares about the punch line when it's delivered.

Two weeks ago, I was late for a keynote address. I raced around the stage area to set up, then maintained that speed throughout the first half of my address. There was hardly a pause. As I rushed through my presentation, the audience members sat there stone-faced. Suddenly, I realized I was giving themno time to process what I was saying, no time to respond. When I slowed down for the second half of the program, the audience soon became involved. My timing and tempo had greatly improved.

Good timing comes only by doing a certain training program again and again. That's why it's frequently the first skill to get rusty when we haven't trained in a certain content area for a while.

In many ways, training is like a conversation. We must give the other parties an opportunity to get involved and contribute, or we soon become a bore. Even if their contribution is merely laughter, a sigh, a groan, or applause, we must give them a chance to respond.

Try videotaping yourself and observing your timing
to experience this concept firsthand!

WARM-UP

-Breaking the Ice-

No late-night talk show would think about going on the air without a warm-up. Trainers shouldn't consider doing so, either.

My friend Pat Hazell has worked as a warm-up act for many of the current television comedies. In writing this book, I interviewed him about his experiences in this line of work. He told me that 15 minutes before the filming of a show, he'd step out in front of the audience members and welcome them, seeking to accomplish these two goals:

- To get the audience—a group of individuals—to feel like a single unit

- To make the audience feel like part of the team that's about to record a successful program

He'd begin with some small talk and jokes, believing that sharing the common experiences of laughter and interaction causes audience members to feel like a unit. He then would introduce the main star of the show. As the star talked with the audience and showed **vulnerability**, the audience began to feel more and more like part of the star and cast's "team."

Unfortunately, there aren't enough training warm-up acts to go around; trainers have to do their own warm-ups—ideally 15 minutes before the session's scheduled start time. If the trainer merely starts the session on time, it's too late. Here's what I try to do. Fifteen minutes or so before the official start of the session, I walk around the room and meet the early participants individually. Then, with about five minutes to go, I place a project or brainteaser transparency on the overhead for table teams to work on. A prize **giveaway** is offered to tables that successfully complete the assignment.

I'm amazed at the difference this warm-up makes! I no longer feel the energy loss that occurs when early attendees sit and read the newspaper. When the official starting time arrives, I find myself facing a group of participants that, at the very least, is sympathetic toward me as I begin the session. At best, the initial inertia has been overcome and we're rolling!

Occasionally, I'll find myself among a group of early arrivals that seem cold or distant. In those cases, I grab a box of rubber bands and distribute them, table by table, 15 minutes before the official start of the session. The participants invariably make some comment about shooting the rubber bands, and I banter back. When I begin the session by having them learn a magic trick using the rubber bands, we're off and running!

I now plan my warm-ups as thoroughly as I plan my sessions. Give it a try!

OPENING

-Bridging to the Audience-

Why do all late-night talk shows begin with a monologue? Why not just begin by introducing the first guest? Write your responses in the space below.

_____

_____

_____

When I began dissecting the opening moments of talk shows, I watched dozens of opening monologues and noticed some patterns. I was surprised to observe that 90 percent of the content in opening monologues concerns subjects already on the minds of audience members. The shows' writers seem to consistently shape the content of opening monologues by asking three primary questions. The first is:

What topics is the audience already thinking about?

Radio, newspaper, and television reporting gets people thinking and talking about certain people and events. Successful comedians build their monologues on those newsworthy personalities and stories. They begin their shows by meeting audience members where they are—by building on scenarios already familiar to them. Then the writers ask:

What experiences do all audience members share?

Monologues that focus on topics such as relationships, family issues, and political or celebrity news help create a sense of **audience participation.** The host continues the process begun in the **warm-up**, working to transform the audience from individual members into a single unit. Reminding them of their commonality accomplishes just that. Later, the host attempts to bridge the audience's thoughts to include the show's guests and other features. The opening monologue isn't the time for this, however; it's too soon.

What self-revelation can the host make that will help the audience identify with him or her?

This is the third major "shaping" question asked by the writers. They know that if the host appears to be revealing something, they'll be building on a strong **intrinsic interest** of the audience. Almost without exception, audience members want an answer to the question, "What is this person really like?" The writers also use the powerful technique of **vulnerability** by having the host reveal personal information to the audience.

I've also noticed, however, that unless it's done tongue-in-cheek, talk-show hosts never self-reveal about their exorbitant salaries or extravagant lifestyles. In other words, don't expect to hear much about their chauffeured limousine ride to the studio. They avoid such details like the plague. These individuals understand that when the audience no longer shares an **identification** with them, their careers are over.

I recently attempted to write an opening for a training session using the preceding three questions. The subject was customer service. A large national chain had just opened in the city in which I was speaking. In need of some supplies, I had visited the new store just that afternoon and was assisted by two clerks with very different attitudes. The **contrast** between the two clerks and their approaches to customer service made a wonderful opening story. All of my participants were quite aware of the store's grand opening; everyone could identify with the experience of interacting with clerks during a shopping trip; and I revealed myself as I talked about my response to each of the clerks. The participants were with me from the beginning. The talk-show formula worked *for* me just as it had worked *on* me!

Try the "monologue formula" the next time you plan
an opening. It's already proven its effectiveness with
millions of people!

CLOSING

-Bringing Down the Curtain-

How do talk-show hosts and actors end their shows? Imagine the following scenario.

You've just seen a wonderful production of *A Christmas Carol*. The cast, returning to the stage for the customary curtain call, receives a well-deserved standing ovation. As the curtain comes down, you turn to leave, well-satisfied with the performance. Suddenly, the actor who played Scrooge bursts through the curtain and calls out, "Don't forget, we're presenting *The Music Man* in January!"

What's your reaction to this announcement?

Trainers do this type of thing to participants all the time. After an appropriate closing, filled with the celebration of a successfully completed training class, a trainer might say, "Don't forget to turn in your evaluations!" or "Don't forget the training session scheduled for next month!"

> Plan your closing moments so that when you close,
> *you close*. Avoid last-minute, anticlimactic
> announcements. Take care of potential "closing
> killers" before delivering your actual, final closing!

REHEARSAL

-Putting the Pieces Together-

Do you remember when you first learned to drive a car with a manual transmission? Push in the clutch, move the stick, then let out the clutch while stepping on the gas. Before you got the flow of these movements down pat, the car too often jerked forward, sputtering to a stop. With practice, you learned to perform the steps automatically, at last giving your attention to the traffic around you.

Now think for a moment about the components a professional singer must coordinate—the melody, the words, the volume, standing position, movement, and microphone handling. And that's not counting the audience members and what they might be feeling. The best singers practice without an audience until they get the mechanical necessities down without thinking. Ultimately, that's the purpose of rehearsals. Then, during the performance, they can give themselves completely to the audience. Singers who haven't spent adequate time rehearsing appear to be singing to themselves, with the audience merely a group of onlookers.

Magicians face the same challenge. A magician who wants to make a handkerchief vanish must initially learn the mechanics. "First, I make my hand into a fist, then I poke the handkerchief into the top of my fist. Next, I execute a 'secret move' to make the handkerchief disappear, and finally, I open my hand to show that it's empty."

Pity the audience where the magician hasn't mastered the mechanics. The audience members feel like voyeurs—watching someone painfully, mechanically going through a magic trick step by step. Due to the magician's necessary focus of attention, s/he is unable to connect with the audience. There's no relationship with the audience due to the performer's preoccupation.

Theater directors understand the components of successful rehearsal. Consequently, play practice is divided into sessions dedicated to read-throughs (for working on lines), blocking (for working on motion and stage movements), rehearsals (for combining the two), and finally, dress rehearsals (for performing the finished product as though for an audience). The hope is that by opening night, the mechanics will have been mastered so that the performers can focus on the audience members and where they are in relation to them.

Trainers experience this same process when beginning a new course. There's so much to remember, so much to do. Unfortunately, connecting with the participants is too often way down on the list of priorities. The trainer who masters the mechanics of presenting the course content acquires the freedom to interact on a deeper level with participants. The learning experience becomes a richer one for all involved.

Rehearsals speed up this process. Trainers who are willing to spend some private time in the training room walking through the process, will be able to connect with participants earlier in the course's evolution.

For me, the first—and possibly most important—rehearsal happens in my mind. As I sit with my course outline in front of me, I visualize myself in the training room, moving through each stage of the course. Where will I stand? How will people react? Where are the props that I'll use? During this mental rehearsal, a myriad of details surfaces. To make sure I remember them, I busily take notes in the margins of my outline.

After that exercise, I enter the training room to arrange my accessories for the course. I enjoy doing this the night before. I put materials out **backstage** to help me remember the order and flow of the course; just a glance at one of my tables helps me recapture them. Finally, I move through the more troublesome sections of the course—the ones that are either complicated due to the number of components or intricate in terms of **routining**. Then I'm ready to give myself to the most important components in any training room—my participants.

Try rehearsing your seminar. You'll enjoy the
freedom it brings!

THE PARTICIPANTS

SECURITY

-Lowering the Emotions-

A psychologist friend of mine enjoys using the following diagram to depict insecurity.

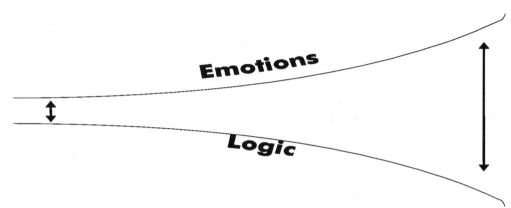

You can sense the power of this diagram by imagining someone coming to within inches of your face and angrily shouting an accusation. Can't you almost feel your emotions rise and, proportionately, your capacity for logic decrease? If, in this condition, you were suddenly called on to caluclate a simple math problem, it would be more difficult than usual in light of your aggravated emotional state. I know I don't think as well when I'm feeling this way.

On the other hand, security looks more like this:

Emotions

Logic

The emotions have come down, allowing the logic to come up. The two components are now free to intertwine throughout the learning experience. The emotions inspire the logic, while the logic acts as a control on the emotions.

Whenever I walk into a new training setting, my insides look much more like the first diagram than the second one. "What will people think of me? Will they like my contributions? How do I compare to others?" are among the questions that arise in my mind in untested situations. To be truly present in a new training environment, I need help to feel like the second diagram. Three components can take me there, and they all involve stability.

The stability of the trainer is foremost. My emotions must be able to relax with him or her. An insecure trainer keeps my emotions from relaxing. A secure trainer is in command of both content knowledge and presentational details. Adequate **rehearsal** causes this person to project confidence.

The stability of the people around me is the second component. My emotions must be able to relax with them. A nonthreatening icebreaker or project gives me a chance to test the interpersonal environment to make sure I'm unlikely to be hurt.

The third component is *the stability of the agenda.* I must know the general direction the training is headed so my emotions can relax with what's to come. **Unpredictability** must occur only within the confines of agenda **predictability.**

I'm unable to truly learn (that is, give myself to the content) until I feel secure in the learning environment.

Talk shows adhere to the following guidelines to assure audience security.

- Adequate **rehearsal** maintains the security of the host.

- A **warm-up** gets the audience comfortable with the host, and vice versa.

- Announcing the agenda several times during the **opening** moments of the show lets everyone know what's to come.

- Using the same general format each evening creates a sense of familiarity with the show.

- An opening monologue helps earn the audience's initial trust by revealing the hotst's **personality, vulnerability, identification,** and **passion**.

These techniques keep participants secure, too. Try
a few the next time you train!

PUBLICITY

-Building Expectations-

I have a friend who performs a mind-reading act in which he appears to tell people in the audience what they're thinking. At one point in the program, he'll say to an audience member, "You are going to receive a phone call from a friend this coming week. The friend will be calling to tell you some very good news!"

"How can you possibly make a prediction like that with the conviction that it'll actually come true?" I asked him.

" 'Self-fulfilling prophecy' and 'selective recall' always work in my favor," my friend replied.

The relationship between these two psychological components is explored more fully in my audiotape titled *Training Secrets from a Psychic.* To understand the implications of these components in the preceding case, it's only necessary to know that the performer projected expectations about the future into the mind of the audience member (by saying, "You are going to receive a phone call from a friend this coming week"). *Self-fulfilling prophecy* means that the audience member will look for that phone call until it's found. Before the performer made the prediction, the audience member would have thought nothing about such a phone call; now, s/he's looking for it.

Selective recall means that the audience member will virtually ignore all phone calls that don't bring good news from a friend and will focus on the call that fulfills the prophecy.

Now let's see what role publicity plays in shaping these two components.

Can you remember what first compelled you to tune into the late-night talk show that's now your favorite? A friend's comment or recommendation? A newspaper or magazine article about the host? A television commercial advertising the show? What expectations did you have when you first tuned in?

_____

_____

_____

Do you recall whether your initial expectations of the show were met? Are your current expectations different from or the same as your initial ones? If they're different, in what way? What factors shaped your modified expectations? The more accurately preshow publicity reflected the true nature of the program, the less disappointed you were and the more likely you were to retain your initial expectations.

The same is true in training. Our participants form expectations about our training even before entering the training room. Due to those expectations, they come looking for certain qualities (self-fulfilling prophecy) and often ignore all other components to ensure that their expectations are met (selective recall).

This phenomenon can work for us or against us. Participants who enter your training room believing they're going to have a terrible experience probably will and may even be able to enumerate specific reasons for their disappointment. They might even become **hecklers**! However, if they come believing it's going to be a great time of learning and growth, they'll probably find it to be so and may be able to specify ways in which it was a worthwhile experience.

Publicity makes the difference. Your pretraining publicity—both printed and word of mouth—shapes expectations and builds anticipation.

> What expectations are generated by your training
> publicity? Are they positive? Realistic?

PACING

-Feeling the Passage of Time-

Although we know that time passes at the same rate every moment of every day, it sure doesn't seem like it. The actual speed at which training content is delivered is called **tempo**; participants' subjective sense of how quickly or slowly time passes during training is called *pacing*.

Watch a late-night talk show and take special note of the segments that seem to pass slowly for you. Which seem to pass most quickly? Are there any common denominators among the segments that seem to pass slowly (the times you're tempted to turn the channel)? Among those that pass quickly?

Every time I perform this experiment, I arrive at the same conclusions. Time passes quickest for me when:

- The subject under discussion interests me.

- I'm involved in the content mentally, emotionally, and sometimes even physically.

Furthermore, I've observed that the less **intrinsic interest** participants have in the content, the more I must involve them physically in it. Take a moment to check out the **audience involvement** section for some practical ideas on how to physically involve participants in even the driest content.

There are few greater feelings during a seminar than when participants look at their watches and announce with disbelief, "I had no idea it was this late already!"

Pick up the pace by involving your participants.
They'll thank you!

INTRINSIC INTERESTS

-Building on the Present-

W hat concerns your participants more than your training content? Psychologist A.H. Maslow's Hierarchy of Needs provides some answers.

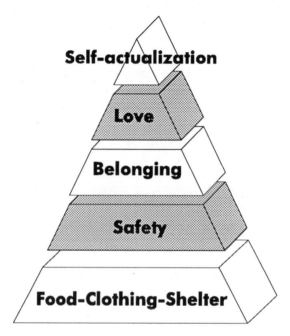

Maslow's studies reveal that at the most foundational level, people are focused primarily on food, clothing, and shelter, followed closely by safety. A sense of belonging precedes the need to be loved, and self-actualization forms the pinnacle of the pyramid. Maslow believed that people concentrate on achieving satisfaction of one need level before moving to the next higher level of the pyramid.

At what level of the pyramid would you guess the typical late-night talk show functions? Why? How do these shows address the need levels *below* that usual functioning level?

Although it leans toward oversimplification, this pyramid can help us understand generational differences. The generation of the Depression grew up concentrating almost entirely on making sure that deprivation never happened to them—or their families—again. Most of their lives were spent trying to satisfy the bottom three levels of Maslow's pyramid. The children of this generation, on the other hand, were raised in relative affluence and have had the luxury of concentrating on the top three levels: belonging, love, and self-actualization.

Training content can be presented at any of these levels. At the lowest level, participants are motivated to take the training to keep their jobs and provide themselves and/or their families with food, clothing, and shelter (first-level needs).

In some companies where I've conducted in-houses, it appeared many employees took training to protect their emotional safety. Intimidation, guilt, and other oppressive tactics seemed to be the managerial norms in these organizations.

Content presented at the "belonging" level places strong emphasis on interpersonal relationships and networking among the participants, bridging to the level of love, with all of its components—i.e., respect, **vulnerability**, and praise.

Finally, content presented within the framework of self-actualization emphasizes the personal growth and development of individual participants as well as the group.

At what level of the pyramid do most of your participants function? If they feel unsafe or vulnerable in your training room, you'll waste your breath trying to approach them on the level of self-actualization. Likewise, if they feel isolated or alienated from the group, the wise trainer will address their "belonging" need before moving to a higher level of functioning.

At what level of the pyramid does your training
room typically function? How do you address needs
below that functioning level?

This page and the next two pages have been

secretly inserted into this book

so that you can perform the magic trick called

Putting It All Together!

as described in the Appendix of this book.

AUDIENCE PARTICIPATION

-Involving Your Participants-

Company policies...statistics...company history. These topics furrow the brow of every conscientious trainer. Although management wants them covered, the experienced trainer intuitively understands that participants usually feel very little need for training sessions on such topics. We're sometimes tempted to start those sessions with an apology—"I'm sorry I have to put you through the next few hours. I guess we can all be glad this happens only once a year! Bear with me, OK?"—but deep down, we feel there must be a better way.

We watch the best of the late-night talk shows keep their studio audiences involved with prizes, giveaways, and banter between the host and guests. But how can we keep participants involved in even the driest topics?

Through the little-known training technique of forecasting, there's hope even for potentially dull content areas. Here's how this technique might be applied to each of the topics mentioned earlier.

Company Policies

To use forecasting to train on the subject of company policies, begin the session by distributing true/false work sheets to participants. Instruct them to circle the correct response for each item, warning that you've sprinkled the list with bogus policies.

PICK THE POLICY

For each item, circle either **True** or **False** to indicate whether the statement describes an actual company policy.

True **False** 1. Employees are allowed 10 sick days per calendar year.

True **False** 2. Employees get their birthdays off every fourth year after working for the company five years.

For maximum enjoyment and energy, include in your list actual company policies, obviously false (and potentially humorous) policies, and items that sound like they might be policies but aren't. Have participants work together as table teams to complete this assignment. Then go through the sheet with them, presenting the policies the company wants you to cover. The participants will hardly know you're training them as you create an atmosphere of fun and competition!

Statistics

Using the statistical-training process of forecasting, create a handout formatted as a two-column work sheet. The left-hand column consists only of numbers, with the right-hand column containing descriptive statements about those numbers (but not in the correct order). Challenge participants to draw lines matching the numbers in the left-hand column with their descriptions on the right.

STATISTICAL SURPRISE!

Draw a line connecting each statistic in the left-hand column with its description in the right-hand column.

1. 950	a. The total number of workers in the warehouse.
2. 3	b. The total dollar amount paid in bonuses to employees last year.
3. 1905	c. The year our company sold its first product.

To enhance the chances for humorous guesswork, put only numbers (e.g., 950) in the left-hand column. Don't indicate what each number signifies. Make participants guess: 950 ducks? 950 people? 950 degrees? This will cause the participants to have a much more difficult time guessing which item in the right hand column corresponds to the number in the left hand column.

After allowing the table teams time to forecast, take them through the work sheet and provide the correct answers so they can see which table did best.

Company History

With company history, the process of forecasting can be twofold. By separating the identification of specific events from the chronology of those events, you can generate variety and greater interaction in the training session.

The true/false format works well for identifying specific events (see the preceding Company Policies section for details). As suggested earlier, compose your list using actual historical events, some obviously funny and phony events, and a sprinkling of events that might have happened but didn't.

HISTORY IN THE MAKING

For each item, circle either **True** or **False** to indicate whether the statement describes an actual event in the history of this company.

True   **False**   1. Walt Disney played a key role in the establishment of this company in 1926.

True   **False**   2. Our current offices were converted from a fast-food franchise in 1986.

True   **False**   3. The company's first sale was made on June 4, 1955.

After they complete the work sheets, guide participants in scoring their table's work by providing the correct answers to the items on the true/false work sheet.

Moving on to the chronological exercise, have table members write the true major events from the true/false work sheet on index cards—one event per card. Then, with the table teams working on the table or floor, instruct them to place their index cards end to end so they accurately reflect the chronological order of those events.

While the tables are working on that task, you can be stringing a rope across the front of the room and setting out larger (pre-prepared) versions of the index cards the teams used for recording major company events. Armed with spring clothespins, you're ready for the tables to take turns trying to pin the large cards on the rope—in chronological order, from left to right. If a team hangs some cards out of order, indicate this (without identifying the errors), then take them all down. Continue to let teams try until one gets the order correct. Prizes for everyone would be a nice touch!

Any training topic involving a list has the potential to be predictable, boring, and uninvolving. This is exactly the type of topic for which forecasting works best!

AUDIENCE ENERGY

-Managing a Limited Supply-

The next time you watch a comedian work with a live audience, try ignoring the comedian and focusing on the audience. Pay particular attention to its bursts of laughter. You'll find that applause and laughter typically take the form of a bell-shaped curve.

The energy of the applause or laughter begins slowly, gains speed, crests, then tapers off.

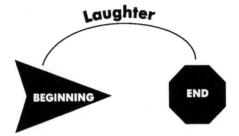

Then listen to the audience *and* watch the performer. Does the performer allow the audience to complete the full curve? Where does the performer jump in and "put a cork" in the group's laughter? Skilled performers begin talking somewhere shortly after the crest of the curve, stopping the audience from ever completing it.

Highly skilled comedians are able to *get on a roll*, building their jokes around a single setup and several punch lines. They'll jump in shortly after the crest of the curve with yet another punch line. This won't stop the release of the audience's energy but will actually heighten it, taking it to yet another level.

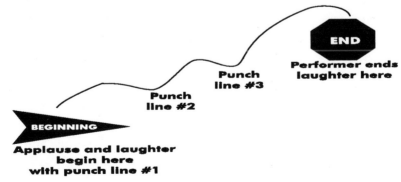

This is what comedians refer to as getting on a roll.

In the book *Tricks for Trainers, Volume 2*, I suggest a prize giveaway for trainers to use with a volunteer: "You've just won a brand new Cadillac (pause) wind-shield (pause) wiper (pause) blade (pause) box (pause) top!" The participant receives a tiny piece of cardboard from the top of a wiper-blade box! With the appropriate pauses, the trainer cuts into the group's laughter and takes the collective energy to yet another level.

Experienced performers (and trainers) understand that any audience brings a limited amount of energy to a performance. This fact has nothing to do with the skill level of the performer. It's true of any group. Throughout the presentation, however, the skilled performer preserves and replenishes that limited energy supply. By not allowing the audience to fully satisfy itself in relation to laughter and applause, the performer conserves—even heightens—the group's energy.

Let's return to the first diagram and change the word *laughter* to *discussion*. Now, applications to the training room are more apparent. If you diagram the energy flow from the moment you turn your participants lose on a discussion topic, you'll find their energy starts slowly, rises, crests, then descends.

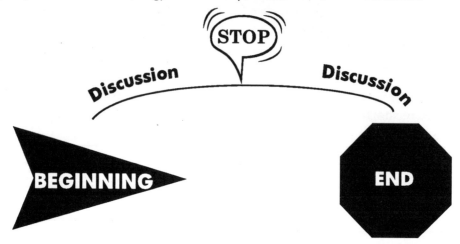

Jump in and stop them when you feel it crest, and you'll conserve their energy. If you ever let them discuss a topic until they are fully satisfied, you'll feel an energy drain in the room that will likely make future discussions difficult. If you feel they could fully discuss a topic in five minutes, give them two!

Unfortunately, that bell-shaped curve also can reflect the energy flow of an entire training session. Participants might start strong, crest, then feel their energy diminish until they almost crawl out of the room at session's end.

It's possible, however, to put together a training session that looks more like the second diagram (the one with the multiple punch lines). By inserting content-oriented activities and energizers at each energy crest, you instill a feeling of progression as the session moves from one level to the next.

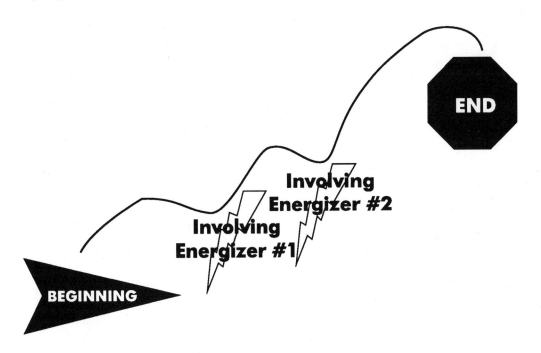

May this diagram increasingly reflect your own
training experience!

PROPS

-Using the Tangible to Illustrate the Intangible-

Why do charities have poster children? Wouldn't it be just as effective to distribute printed flyers with statistics indicating how many people have the disease and how many have been cured? Of course not! Through the use of one poster child, a charity can make the intangible nature of statistics very tangible.

Although it isn't the intent of this author to make a comparison between a disabled child and the use of props in the training room, the principle of using the dramatic to make a point does have a powerful application to the communication of content.

When dealing with the intangible, look for a prop that can help make it tangible. If the topic is customer service, why not use the following story?

A consultant was hired to evaluate why a certain candy store was losing customers while the one right across the mall was flourishing. She observed both operations and listened to customers talk when leaving the establishments.

Based on those observations, the consultant learned the following. In the store that was failing, the clerk would put some candy on the scale, then take some away until the weight exactly matched what the customer had ordered. The customers left complaining about how the store took candy away from them. In the other store, the clerk put a little candy on the scale, then kept adding small amounts until the weight equalled the amount ordered. Customers left that store feeling like the clerk had *added* candy to their orders.

After listening to customers' comments at both stores, the consultant suggested a change in the way the failing store dispensed its candy. The clerk would first put a little candy on the scale, then ask if the customer had tried the new strawberry-flavored candy yet. If not, the clerk would give the customer a sample. While the customer sampled the piece of candy, the clerk would keep adding candy to the scale, a little at a time, until it reached the amount originally ordered. The clerk would then put the candy in a nice box and place a chocolate turtle on top as an added bonus. The cost of the two pieces of candy given away was negligible compared to the customers' perception of value received. The candy store's business increased dramatically!

After telling that story, you're ready to brainstorm with your group similar applications pertaining to their industry or company.

Finally, open a box of wrapped hard candies and give all participants in your training room one to keep in their pocket for 30 days. They are not to eat it; they should simply keep it in their pocket to remind them of the story and the power of giving the customer that little extra. Warn them that employees can check up on each other at anytime. The one who's found without his or her piece of candy owes the other a cup of coffee. You've just used a prop (a piece of candy) to make an intangible (effective customer service) very tangible!

An additional benefit of props can be seen by watching a late-night talk show and noting the increased **audience energy** when props are introduced. Even though it may be only a picture, an ad, or an article, you can feel the audience leaning forward in anticipation of what's about to occur.

The **Attention Management** section explains the dynamics of what occurs when a prop is introduced: We always watch the newest component introduced into an environment—it's automatic! If a talk-show host holds something up, shows interest in it, moves it, points to it, then makes a comment about it, we can hardly resist giving it our focus. Props are a great tool for focusing attention and increasing audience energy.

When the prop is unusual, a trainer can additionally tap into participants' curiosity—that very powerful aspect of **conflict/resolution**. In the book *Tricks for Trainers, Volume 2,* there is a photo of a black-and-white wheel that becomes very colorful when spun. I removed the blades from an old household fan and attached this wheel in its place. This "wheel fan" sits up in front of the room from the beginning of my training sessions and never fails to generate questions. By the time I finally bring the group's curiosity to resolution by using the wheel to illustrate a content point, the power of that prop has skyrocketed! Selecting an unusual prop and using it to build curiosity heightens learning impact.

Pick a prop...build curiosity...use the prop to
illustrate content. It's a winning combination!

PRINTED PROGRAMS

-Explaining the Unwieldy-

Have you been to the ballet lately? Upon entering the theater, an usher hands you a printed program describing the performance you're about to see. Those who attend plays receive a similar type of booklet.

Have you read *TV Guide* recently? That's television's version of the printed program. Sometimes, you'll find only guest listings for your favorite talk shows; other times, there might be a feature article about the host.

The last time I attended the ballet, I observed that while some people never even opened their printed programs, others pored over them until the house lights went down. And I must confess that I've watched many hours of television without reading the program notes in *TV Guide*. So, I ask myself: What purpose do printed programs serve?

This book's **Clarity** chapter explicitly instructs trainers to ruthlessly eliminate any "nice to know" content from their presentations. Clarity demands that training sessions present only those pieces of information participants must know in order to master the content.

So, what becomes of the nonessential, "nice to know" material? It's assembled into a handy printed program. Just as ballet attendees and talk-show viewers don't need a program or a *TV Guide*, training participants don't require the "nice to know" material to realize benefits. For those so inclined, however, the information is there in the program.

Assembling the "nice to know" material from your content into a program produces three benefits. First, you won't feel as compelled to clutter your presentation with nonessentials, since you know your participants will have access to them. Second, you're providing enriching information to participants who'd like to pursue your theme further. And finally, a printed program allows you to enhance your image of **prestige** with participants while avoiding the pitfall of presenting too much content during the training session. It shows them how much more you know about the subject than the class time allowed you to share.

Put your content in print. Think of how much print
has impacted you!

GIVEAWAYS

-Giving the Unexpected-

A national sporting-supply outlet began at a kitchen table in my home state of Nebraska. A husband and wife produced handmade fishing flies and sold them through ads in sports magazines. Their first ad read:

---

12 Fishing Flies
$1.00

(postage/handling included)

The ad also included their name and post-office box for mailing in orders. Unfortunately, the orders didn't come. The couple grew more discouraged with each passing month. Before quitting, they made one significant change to their ad. Here's the revised version:

FREE!
12 Fishing Flies

($1.00 postage/handling)

And the rest is history! The company now mails hundreds of thousands of sporting-goods catalogs around the world annually. We love receiving anything *free*!

Talk shows give away T-shirts, caps, dinner coupons—even canned hams. They create great audience energy with their distribution. The giveaways are definitely added value, since no one expected anything free for going to the show (see **The Encore** and **Unpredictability** for more in-depth exploration of these themes).

Two guidelines seem to be observed by the talk shows in ensuring the effectiveness of giveaways. First, seldom is everyone in the audience given something.

Limiting the number of giveaways seems to increase the value of each one (see **The Ticket**). If you want everyone in your session to receive something extra, this principle indicates it's better to use a variety of giveaway items than to give everyone the same thing.

Second, the person who receives a giveaway typically does something to "earn" it. On a talk show, the person might participate in a stunt, answer a question correctly, or play a game. You might try doing a giveaway when a participant turns in a course evaluation, answers a review question correctly, or wins in a drawing. This earning of the giveaway appears to increase the giveaway's value to that recipient.

Test these guidelines with your own giveaways and
experience the difference!

THE TICKET

-Limiting Availability-

What makes some tickets so valuable? Lots of people wait in line all night just to be there when the box office opens. Others pay premium prices to "scalpers" outside the arena or stadium the night of the event.

Does the fact that there's a limited number available add to a ticket's value? How would things be different if there were an endless supply? Scarce tickets become valuable because we know that not everyone will be able to get one. We'll be special...our friends might envy us!

There's a bakery in my hometown that operates on Main Street out of the owners' home. Although I've never been there, I'm getting closer and closer to making the stop. This business has a Sold Out sign in its window by noon on any given day. For all I know, they make and sell only three rolls a day. But I do know that people driving by can't help wondering what they're missing!

When I travel to conferences, I know that once my supply of books gets down to 10, we're sure to sell out. As those books are sold, we simply mention to the buyers that they've purchased one of the last 10 available. Others then flock around, wanting to purchase that which is almost gone. A sense of urgency is generated and a greater perceived value given to the remaining books.

I recently addressed a group of new car dealers who were preparing to launch a statewide advertising promotion. Every dealer had been mailed two Gold Kits for a certain model of car. Each of these kits contained gold name plates, trim, and a hood ornament and sold to the dealer for less than $200. The dealers could apply these accessories to cars on their lots. The only rule was that there must never be more than two cars with this kit on the lot at any given time. When this rule was followed, statistics proved that the two "gold cars" sold quickly. The dealer could then purchase two more kits, apply them to two more cars, and generate even more sales. The Gold Kit made a car special. Ensuring that no more than two cars had the kit at any one time made those cars appear very limited indeed.

This same technique of showmanship has applications in the training room, too. For instance, when using **giveaways**, you can increase their value by not having enough for everyone. That automatically causes each giveaway to have a greater perceived value. Likewise, you might consider ways in which people must qualify for your training courses (prerequisites, etc.). If that were possible, it would give those who attend your courses greater **prestige**.

You can also provide an incentive by offering premiums to the first 10 people to sign up for the course or the first seven people back from lunch and in their seats—anything to signal limited availability of anything!

You might even consider having tickets printed for your course. Although they wouldn't cost participants anything, they would begin building anticipation when mailed out. Using the tickets in a drawing is another way of giving them purpose and ensuring that participants brought them to class.

> Limiting an item's availability makes people want it
> more. Try it in your training!

ATTENTION MANAGEMENT

-Obtaining and Maintaining Participant Attention-

The next time you watch a performer or trainer, try to identify when one of the following techniques from Darwin Ortiz's excellent book, *Strong Magic*, is being used. Each of these eight techniques takes control of the audience's attention, then directs it to wherever the performer desires.

The presenter's own interest. A performer (trainer) who's not interested in the subject will have great difficulty involving the audience. Performers can show that interest by looking at the focal point, and the audience follows their eyes. As a trainer, you'll find one exception to this rule: When you want participants to look at you, look at them!

The presenter's gestures. If I point at an object or a person, it's extremely difficult for participants not to follow with their eyes. It's one characteristic that separates people from animals. Point in front of a dog, and the dog looks at your finger; point in front of a group of people, and thy follow your point. Couple this gesture with the aforementioned glance and, you have a winning combination!

The presenter's words. If you look, point, and then use words to direct the audience, you add the auditory component to the mix and strengthen the impact even more.

The presenter's movement. We watch that which is in **motion**. If you've been standing still for a while and begin to move, your participants will watch you. If you move an object, they'll follow it with their eyes.

Sound. We watch whatever is making noise.

Contrast. We watch anything that's different from its surroundings— in color, size, shape, etc. If it's in contrast, we'll focus on it!

Newness. We watch whatever arrived last. If it's the newest visual on the scene, it has our attention. The longer something is in our sight, the less attention we give it.

Intrinsic interests. Finally, each of us has certain topics, objects, and people in which we have **intrinsic interest.** We'll automatically watch if one of them is in view.

The best attention-management style uses a combination of these eight techniques at once. If I bring out an intrinsically interesting **prop** that is either very large or very small, look at it, point at it, move it, have it make a sound, and then make a comment about it, I've combined all eight techniques. Without a doubt, the participants' attention will be on that prop!

If, in addition to applying these techniques, I've made sure to minimize any distractions in the surrounding scenery or in relation to the participants (e.g., **hecklers**), I will have maximized the effectiveness of those techniques.

Experiment with various technique combinations until you know with absolute certainty that you can get the attention and direct the focus of your participants anytime you want to.

**This knowledge will add immensely to
your training confidence!**

HECKLERS

-Managing Problematic Participants-

They come in all shapes and sizes. Sometimes you can see it in their eyes; sometimes they sneak up on you. I'm talking about training participants who resent your being in control: hecklers.

The techniques hecklers use to wrest control from trainers range from the brazen rudeness of reading a newspaper or conversing with peers during the training session to the more subtle tactic of continually asking questions or making comments. In either case, what's a trainer to do? When heckling occurs, one or more of the following 11 possibilities might exist.

Misinterpretation of a participant's intentions. Some trainers insist on having absolute, autocratic control of their training sessions. In this scenario, an honest comment or normal give-and-take between the trainer and a participant can be viewed as heckling. The trainer then assumes a defensive posture, and the crisis escalates.

*Trainer's low **prestige** in eyes of participants.* In this case, trainees haven't been made aware of the trainer's credentials; consequently, they don't treat him or her with due respect.

Trainer's lack of respect for him- or herself. Self-respect breeds respect from others. Trainers who have little respect for themselves allow participants to walk all over them. It's a sad scene.

*Trainer's obnoxious **personality**.* Participants don't have a corner on obnoxiousness; trainers can exhibit it, too. Trainers who treat participants in a condescending or disrespectful manner will eventually find themselves facing a group of combative trainees.

*Inappropriate training **tempo**.* If the course is moving too slowly, there will be an energy vacuum that someone will try to fill in an effort to alleviate boredom.

Lack of adequate breaks. If the trainer doesn't provide enough breaks, participants will create their own.

Overfamiliarity. A plaque reading "Familiarity breeds contempt" should hang on every trainer's office wall. By allowing your familiarity with participants to go beyond a polite, friendly business level, you risk increased difficulty maintaining control. This has to do with the appropriateness of jokes you tell, the topics you discuss, and kidding done by you and with you. You may have trouble defining the line before you cross it; after crossing it, however, you'll realize quickly that you've overstepped the boundary. The sooner you return to the other side of the line, the better it will be for both you and your group.

Trainer's too-casual **costuming.** Typically speaking, the more casual a trainer's clothing, the harder it will be for him or her to maintain control of the group. Casual clothes silently signal an informal, unstructured situation. This is the opposite of a situation in which control is easily managed. A good rule of thumb is to be dressed at least as formally as your most formally dressed participant.

Inadequate **audience involvement.** If you don't give your participants enough opportunities for self-expression, they'll create their own!

Inadequate **rehearsal.** A trainer who fumbles instead of flows creates insecurity on the part of participants that eventually will be acted out.

A genuinely neurotic participant. This is a participant who has a genuine problem with someone else having any measure of control. In my 20 years of training, I've experienced one of these per every 100 or so participants.

Here's the good news! Trainers can unilaterally solve 90 percent of heckling problems through minor changes in their personal style and approach. If you look again at the preceding list, you'll notice that 10 out of 11 possibilities reflect directly on the trainer. But what about truly troublesome trainees? Although there's no magical solution, here are some approaches I've tried.

Ignore them. Remember, attention is what they want. The first step is to avoid giving it to them. If your ego is not allowed to get involved, you might be able to ignore them until they tire of their antics.

Contain them. By having participants work in small groups, you can contain hecklers so they don't infect the entire class. This method of dividing and conquering helps minimize the damage. Often, the peer group is able to manage the person's tendency to control.

Overwhelm them. This technique works only for certain extroverted trainers. You intensify the speed of the training session and/or your own personality to a degree that dwarfs the personality of the offender. Often, this communicates to the heckler that you are indeed in control. Consequently, the heckler feels more secure and will stop the interruptions.

Involve them. At the next break, invite hecklers to help prepare for upcoming activities. Frequently, being chosen to assist you will make them feel more like they're on your team and increase their willingness to work with you for the remainder of the training.

Confront them. The last resort, this step involves talking to troublesome participants privately about the problem and seeking their cooperation.

A heckler should always cause a trainer to look in
the mirror first and in the heckler's direction only
thereafter.

THE ENCORE

-Adding Value-

Three years ago, a friend of mine attended the stage show of a famous Las Vegas performer for the first time. He came back and reported, in glowing terms, how the performer at one point had remarked to the audience, "This show is running overtime, but since you're such a great audience, I'll do one more song!" The crowd went wild!

After two or three numbers, the performer glanced at his watch again, then said, "The showroom manager must be fit to be tied at how far overtime we've gone now!" Two more songs later, the performer lamented, "We're so far overtime now, I guess it just doesn't matter anymore!" The audience members jumped to their feet, applauding.

When my friend recently returned to Las Vegas, there was no question about it—he had to see this generous performer again. Imagine his surprise when the entertainer used the very same lines to lengthen his show—which ended at exactly the same time as the show my friend had seen three years earlier!

Nevertheless (or possibly because of this "technique"), this performer fills Las Vegas showrooms night after night, year after year. He's learned to use the power of an encore without even waiting for the audience to ask for one. He uses a orm of **planned spontaneity**.

The tactic he uses makes every audience feel special. It gives each show an air of **unpredictability.** Everyone there feels lucky to be a member of the audience that night. The performer knows how to infuse each performance with a sense of immediacy, giving his audience members unexpected added value. That's what we love about encores—the performer gives us a song we wouldn't have received if we hadn't been there that night, jumping to our feet and applauding wildly!

Although late-night talk-show hosts don't do encores, they, too, work—through constantly changing guest lists and special features—to make audience members glad to be there.

So, where does this powerful piece of showmanship fit into the training room? Here are some ideas I have used.

- I have a special activity in my training bag that I pull out on the spur of the moment when I have a very responsive training group.

- When someone makes a comment, I often tie it into my next planned activity as though the person gave me a spur-of-the-moment inspiration.

- I also have a supply of inexpensive **giveaways**—including copies of training articles that I duplicate and distribute in response to questions from specific training groups.

This last idea has proven so popular that I now take a file of articles to every training session. When the members of a group know I went the extra mile for them by duplicating an article during a break, I've tapped into the power of an encore—I've just given them added value.

The next time you train, try an encore!

THE BOW

-Projecting an Attitude-

The next time you see an entertainer take a bow, try to determine what the performer is saying by assuming such a posture. Could it be, "I know I'm good...I'm glad you finally figured it out"? Or, "Thanks for paying me lots of money. Now, get out of here so I can go home"? How about, "You're welcome"?

Now consider another spirit in which people bow. As a gesture of honor and humility, subjects have bowed before kings and queens through the ages. In fact, the bow was originally an attmept of subjects to keep their heads lower than the head of the monarch.

So when performers bow before their audiences (in other than a perfunctory manner), they are saying, "I know I am no better than you. Therefore, I am honored that you would want to take time from your life to watch what Ido and hear what I have to say." Any other attitude hurts the relationship between the performer and the audience—or the trainer and the participants, for that matter. Only with "the attitude of the bow" is the performance placed in its proper perspective.

In the final analysis, training, too, is a gift—brought by the trainer to honor his or her participants.

> And this book is my gift to you. May you apply its
> principles to your content...and then take a bow!

THE APPENDIX

PUTTING IT ALL TOGETHER!

-A Magic Trick You Can Do-

This section presents an easy magic trick designed to help you practice many of the 49 principles of showmanship described in this book.

Imagine this...

Working with a volunteer from your training group, you'll thumb through the pages of this book until the person tells you to stop. Turning your head away so that you can't see, you'll open the book and instruct the volunteer to think of any sentence on either of the two pages in view. You'll then close the book and unerringly identify the exact sentence your volunteer is thinking about. The sentence can even relate to the subject matter of your training, making this trick a great closer!

Here's how to prepare

Turn to the three blank pages toward the end of the book (inserted between pages 84 and 85). Take a pair of scissors and cut the first two pages on the dashed vertical lines so that these pages are slightly narrower than the third page. Then turn to the uncut blank page and neatly print a single sentence on it—preferably, one that has something to do with your content. If your topic is customer service, you might print something like, "Treat customers as you would like to be treated." If you're training on quality, you might print, "There's no substitute for quality." You get the idea.

Now, hold the book by its spine in one hand while using the thumb of your other hand to riffle the pages from front to back. You'll hear a slight "click" when you pass the cut pages. You'll have little problem stopping at the click so that the volunteer is forced to look at the prepared page.

Here's how to do it!

Announce to your training group that you'd like to make an attempt at mind reading (**Intrinsic Interests**). You hope that it'll be successful (**Conflict/Resolution**). However, you'll need help (**Vulnerability**) from someone in the group (**Audience Participation**). When the volunteer joins you at the front of the room (**The Trainer's Stage**), stand side by side, both facing the audience.

Look around as though searching for something, then pretend to suddenly notice this book (**Planned Spontaneity**). Remove the book (**Props**) from its visible but inaccessible location (**Backstage**) and hold it up briefly for all to see (**Attention Management**). Explain that you'll riffle through the pages, waiting for the volunteer to say "stop" (**Clarity**). Then riffle through the pages so quickly that no one could say "stop" fast enough (**Humor**) and offer to slow it down a little. This time, riffle through the book, a little slower, from front to back. When the volunteer says "stop," let the remaining pages fall so that you stop at the click and open the book to the prepared page (**Rehearsal**). Turn your head away and instruct the volunteer to look over the two pages and "think about any sentence on one of the pages" (**Scripting**). Be sure to hold the book so that the other participants cannot see the pages.

Wait a few seconds (**Timing**), then ask if the volunteer has selected a sentence yet. Quickly close the book (**Tempo**) and place it backstage, out of reach. Dramatically step back (**Motion**) and state that you'll now attempt to read your volunteer's mind (**Progression**). Slowly reveal one word in the sentence after another (**Unveiling**), not necessarily in the right order (**Unpredictability**). Make an occasional mistake, then correct yourself (**Identification**). Finally, present the entire sentence from beginning to end (**Conflict/Resolution**).

Accept the group's applause and request a hand for the volunteer (**Audience Energy**). Finally, give the volunteer a book by the Amazing Kreskin as a thank-you for helping (**Giveaway**) and take your bow (**The Bow**).

Note: If you think it might be fun to include simple magic tricks in your training, consider this author's books on the subject: *Tricks for Trainers*, volumes 1 and 2, and *First Impressions/Lasting Impressions*. These are available from the publisher by calling 800-383-9210.

49 PRINCIPLES OF SHOWMANSHIP

SHOWMANSHIP

The art of making the ordinary extraordinary

SHOWMANSHIP

The application of the qualities of presentation usually reserved for the uncommon to the common

THE PRESENTER

PERSONALITY

The trainer's unique combination of positive and negative personal qualities that helps distinguish him or her from other people

CHARACTER DEVELOPMENT

The conscious selection of personality traits that the trainer wishes to share with participants

IDENTIFICATION

The capacity of participants to empathize with the trainer's chosen persona

UNITY

The overall sense that the trainer's vocabulary, movements, clothing, voice, and content selection all fit his or her characterization

THE PRESENTATION

THE TRAINER'S STAGE

The part of the training room designated as the trainer's primary presentation area

BACKSTAGE

The part of the training room that is "off-limits" to participants

COLOR

A silent tool with powerful uses in both attention management and the successful projection of the trainer's chosen persona

SCENERY

A thoughtfully constructed physical backdrop against which the training presentation might effectively occur

PRESTIGE

The respect that derives from the trainer's educational and/or experiential credentials encouraging participants to pay close attention during the training session

VULNERABILITY

The trainer's process of communicating trust by revealing to participants certain aspects of who he or she is

PASSION

The trainer's emotional communication of strong convictions on any given training topic

COSTUMING

The trainer's selection of a wardrobe with a view toward strengthening the projection of his or her chosen training persona

MOTION

The trainer's always-purposeful movement

HUMOR

The trainer's use of laughter as another method of sharing with participants who he or she is

CURRENTNESS

The trainer's nonverbal communication—through wardrobe, vocabulary, and interests—that he or she is up to date as a trainer

MISTAKES

The trainer's use of the emotional tag to cover and recover when an activity does not receive a positive response from participants

CLARITY

The trainer's ruthless elimination of all nonessential content and subsequent delivery of essential content to meet participants where they are

ROUTINING

The trainer's thoughtful ordering of presentational components in keeping with the principles of good showmanship

PROGRESSION

The trainer's ongoing attempt to give a training session the feeling that it's "going somewhere"

FLOW

The trainer's construction of smooth bridges among the various sections of the training session

VARIETY

The trainer's prevention of participant boredom by varying the components of location, music, special features, lighting, and tempo throughout the training session

CONTRAST

The trainer's maintenance of audience interest and involvement by placing both props and entire training sections in opposition to their surroundings

TEMPO

The actual speed at which the trainer delivers content

CONFLICT/ RESOLUTION

The trainer's involvement of participants in the content by capitalizing on a foundational principle of good plot construction

PLANNED SPONTANEITY

The trainer's infusion of the energy of immediacy into a training session through an apparently impromptu action

UNPREDICTABILITY

The trainer's nurturance of the exciting possibility that the unexpected might occur anytime during the training session

PREDICTABILITY

The stabilizing quality that allows unpredictability to occur within the overall familiar format of a training session

MUSIC

A showman's tool that the trainer must use wisely to set expectations, maintain group energy, and establish atmosphere within the training room

UNVEILING

The trainer's process of dramatically revealing a piece of presentational material to the training group

SCRIPTING

The trainer's deliberate selection of the best words for clearly communicating content, involving the participants, and projecting the desired training persona

TIMING

The actual interval of time a trainer lets lapse between two words, two actions, or a spoken word and an action

WARM-UP

The trainer's effort to establish rapport with participants before the actual start of the training session

OPENING

The initial critical moments of training when the trainer makes his or her first impression on participants

CLOSING

The trainer's act of successfully "bringing down the curtain" on a completed training session

REHEARSAL

The trainer's practicing of a training session without participants present

THE PARTICIPANTS

SECURITY

The trainer's plan to help reduce participants' insecurities and fears so that maximum content processing can occur

PUBLICITY

The trainer's effective use of both pre- and postsession publicity to build maximum anticipation and appropriate expectations of the training session

PACING

The participants' subjective sense of the speed at which time is passing during the training session

INTRINSIC INTERESTS

The trainer's involvement of participants in the content by referring to people or topics in which they already have an interest

AUDIENCE PARTICIPATION

The trainer's involvement of participants mentally, emotionally, and physically with content

AUDIENCE ENERGY

The trainer's conservation and replenishment of that which is always in limited supply

PROPS

The trainer's use of the tangible to illustrate the intangible

PRINTED PROGRAMS

The trainer's distribution of printed materials featuring those "nice to know" (nonessential) elements of his or her content

GIVEAWAYS

The trainer's creation of interest and energy by giving participants something unexpected

THE TICKET

The trainer's use of the technique of limiting supply to elevate value

ATTENTION MANAGEMENT

The trainer's use of eight techniques for focusing participants' attention

HECKLERS

The trainer's prevention of the transfer of control from him- or herself to a participant

THE ENCORE

Added value given to participants by the trainer throughout
the training experience

THE BOW

The trainer's projection of "the
attitude of the bow" during
training

THE LATE-NIGHT TALK SHOW TRAINING GUIDE

TOPIC	DISCOVERY QUESTIONS	PAGE
Scenery	Try describing the show's background scenery from memory. Then watch the show and fill in the details. What does the scenic background add to the show?	21

THE SHOW'S HOST

Personality	What aspects of the host's personality make you prefer this show over the other?	3
Character Development	List qualities of the host's persona along with observations that make you believe each is true.	6
Currentness	What about the host makes you believe that he has remained up to date?	35
Costuming	Turn the volume down and concentrate on the hosts clothing. What does it tell you about what the host is like as a person?	30
Scripting	What does the host's choice of words tell you about the host as a person? At what grade level do you believe he speaks?	64
Unity	Compare the personality traits you listed for Character Development, Costuming, and Scripting. How similar or different are the lists?	10

THE SHOW'S OPENING

Warm-Up	Does the host meet with the studio audience before the formal introduction?	68
Prestige	What would be lacking if the host came out with no introduction?	23

TOPIC	DISCOVERY QUESTIONS	PAGE
Unveiling	Why does the host walk out from backstage instead of sitting in the audience and walking onstage?	62
Opening	What key components can you identify in the opening monologue?	70
Identification	How does the host help the audience identify with him?	8
Vulnerability	During the opening monologue, try identifying instances in which the host becomes emotionally vulnerable to the audience.	26
Security	What techniques does the host use to help the audience feel secure?	77
Passion	When does the host express strong emotion during the opening monologue? What does this expression of passion add?	28
Motion	Turn the volume down and watch the host's movements—facial expressions and use of body language. What observations do you make about how the host uses his or her body to communicate?	32
Humor	What do you learn about the host through his humor?	33
Timing	When the host tells jokes, listen for pauses before the punch lines. What difference does timing make in the success or failure of the jokes?	66
Mistakes	When the host's jokes don't go over, what observations do you make about how he recovers?	36
Hecklers	If someone begins shouting out comments from the studio audience, how does the host respond in order to keep control?	101

TOPIC	DISCOVERY QUESTIONS	PAGE
Clarity	What techniques does the host use to ensure his jokes are understood by the majority of the audience?	38
Intrinsic Interests	How many of the jokes in the opening monologue relate to topics already on the minds of audience members?	82
Audience Energy	Listen to the host interrupt the laughter and applause of the audience. Why does he do that?	89

THE SHOW'S CONTENT

TOPIC	DISCOVERY QUESTIONS	PAGE
The Trainer's Stage	How does the feeling of the show change as the host positions himself in different places on the stage?	15
Pacing	Which parts of the show seem to go fast for you and which go slower? Why?	81
Routining	List the parts of the typical routine followed by the show? Why is the order followed night after night?	40
Progression	Does the show feel like it's "going somewhere"? Why or why not?	43
Flow	How smoothly is show going? What gives a show the feeling of smoothness?	45
Variety	How do the show's producers add variety to the show?	47
Contrast	During what parts of the show do you notice the greatest contrast in speed of delivery, content, or volume?	48
Tempo	When does the host speed up the show and when does he move it at a more leisurely pace? Why?	49

AUTHOR BIOGRAPHY

-DAVE ARCH-

As a Senior Trainer for Bob Pike's Creative Training Techniques International, Inc. Dave Arch authored all three books in the Tricks for Trainers Resource Library including *Tricks for Trainers, Volume I & II* as well as *First Impressions/Lasting Impressions.*

In addition, Dave travels for Creative Training Techniques to over twenty cities in the United States each year presenting the seminar Techniques and Tricks. For two days he leads trainers through an experience of 119 attention management techniques as found in his books.

Dave has literally pioneered the use of magic in training. Since 1982, magic has proven itself an effective communication tool for groups as diverse as hospital CEO's to sales representatives to banking administrators.

Combining a ten year background in personal and family counseling with a professional expertise in magic, Dave travels from his home in Omaha, Nebraska, to present his unique presentations before some 25,000 people each year in both corporate and conference settings.

-ROBERT W. PIKE, CSP-

Bob Pike has developed and implemented training programs for business, industry, government, and the professions since 1969. As president of Creative Training Techniques International, Inc., and publisher of Creative Training Techniques Press, Bob spends more than 150 days a year leading sessions on such topics as leadership, attitudes, motivation, communication, decision making, problem solving, personal and organizational effectiveness, conflict management, team building and managerial productivity. More than 60,000 trainers have attended the Creative Training Techniques™ workshop. As a consultant, Bob has worked with such organizations as Pfizer, UpJohn, Caesar Boardwalk Regency, Exhibitor Magazine, Hallmark Cards, and IBM.

Over the years Bob has contributed to magazines including *TRAINING, The Personal Administrator,* and *The Self-Development Journal.* He is editor of the Creative Training Techniques Newsletter and author of *The Creative Training Techniques Handbook* and *Improving Managerial Productivity.*

More great resources from Jossey-Bass/Pfeiffer!

End your sessions with a BANG!

Lynn Solem
& Bob Pike

50 Creative Training Closers

They'll forget you as soon as you walk out the door—unless you make your training memorable. This essential resource is your way to make your mark. Fifty ways to close your training sessions and presentations so they won't forget you—or your training.

Many trainers start training sessions memorably with a rousing icebreaker, or with a spirited overview of what's to follow. But you're probably letting the ends slip through your fingers. Some trainers conclude training sessions by looking at their watches and saying, "Oh, time's up! Goodbye!" By trailing off with a whisper, you're missing an opportunity to reinforce your training. You're helping your participants to forget everything you've taught them. Stop this brain drain by ending with a bang! This invaluable book is packed with practical closers.

You get activities great for:

- *Reviewing* material
- *Celebrating* success
- *Motivating* participants . . . and more!

Solem and Pike show you all the essentials, and preparation is quick and easy. So little time to invest for such a HUGE payoff! This book is training dynamite—make it your secret weapon today.

paperback / 96 pages
....
50 Creative Training Closers
Item #F439

Bob Pike &
Dave Arch

Dealing with Difficult Participants

127 Practical Strategies for Minimizing Resistance and Maximizing Results in Your Presentations

Everyone knows them . . . but almost no one knows how to deal with them. Difficult participants. The "latecomer." The "know-it-all." The "confused." What do you do? Train-the-trainer master Bob Pike and magician/trainer Dave Arch have the answers.

Learn to deal with types such as:

- The Preoccupied
- The Socializer
- The Introvert
- The Bored
- The Domineering
- The Unqualified
- The Skeptic
- The Sleeper . . . and others!

Don't let difficult participants get the best of you. You can't afford not to pick up this engaging book. Maximize the learning potential in all your presentations with *Dealing With Difficult Participants*!

paperback / 150 pages
....
Dealing with Difficult Participants
Item #F244

Bob Pike's
Creative Training Techniques™
Train-the-Trainer Conference

*The only conference dedicated exclusively
to the participant-centered approach to training*

- Learn about the revolutionary, participant-centered training approach—the breakthrough alternative to lecture-based training
- See the nation's leading training consultants model their very best participant-centered activities
- Experience the power of participant-centered techniques to dramatically increase retention
- Learn about innovative training transfer techniques adopted by leading Fortune 500 companies
- Discover powerful management strategies that clearly demonstrate the business results for your training programs

Just a few of the companies who have sent groups (not just individuals) to the Conference

**American Express • AT&T • Caterpillar • First Bank
Southern Nuclear Operating Company • State Farm • United HealthCare • US West**

Rave Reviews!

"I refer to my conference workbook all the time. I've shared the techniques with my trainers, and my own evaluations have improved. Our needs analysis now produces actionable input. My comfort level with our line managers has increased—at my first meeting with them where I used what I learned at the conference, they applauded. Now that's positive feedback!"

Gretchen Gospodarek, Training Manager, **TCF Bank Wisconsin**

"For any trainer who wants to move beyond lecture-based training, I recommend Bob Pike's participant-centered seminars and in-house consultants."

Ken Blanchard, Co-Author of *The One-Minute Manager*

"Bob Pike is creating a new standard in the industry by which all other programs will soon be measured."

Elliott Masie, President, **The MASIE Center**

Visit our Web site: www.cttbobpike.com to learn more about the Conference,
Creative Training Techniques International, Inc. or the Participant-Centered Training approach.

1–800–383–9210
www.cttbobpike.com

Creative Training Techniques International, Inc. • 7620 W. 78th St., Mpls., MN 55439 • 612-829-1954 • Fax 612-829-0260

CREATIVE TRAINING TECHNIQUES

Assisting trainers in achieving exceptional learner satisfaction and bottom-line results using innovative methods, concepts, and technologies is the focus of Bob Pike's Creative Training Techniques Companies.

Building trainer competencies is the goal of Creative Training Techniques International, Inc., the world's largest provider of public and in-house professional-development training. More than 150 seminars covering 40-plus cities are held each year, modeling the best of instructor-led, participant-centered training. Many of the more than 60,000 alumni of this powerful program gather at a refresher conference in Minneapolis each fall.

Bob Pike's popular train-the-trainer offerings include:

- Creative Training Techniques: 37 Ways to Deliver Training with Greater Impact and Effectiveness

- Training for Impact: Needs Assessment, Training Transfer, and Evaluation Methods for Bottom-Line Success

- Creating High Impact Visuals and Interactive Learning Activities: Practical and Proven Graphics & Games for Dynamic Trainers

- High Impact Soft Skills Training: 119 Magical Attention Management and Review Tools to Make Your Sessions More Powerful

For a free catalog of public seminars or for information on in-house sessions, call 800-383-9210 (in the U.S.) or 612-829-1954.

CREATIVE TRAINING TECHNIQUES PRESS

Bob Pike's Creative Training Techniques Press is a convenient source of creative games, graphics, music, how-to books and videos, and presentation tools for enhancing trainer effectiveness. All products are available by phone or mail order, and are completely satisfaction-guaranteed.

Three available trainer-development videos by Bob Pike are *High Impact Presentations,* award winning *Creative Training and Presentation Techniques* and *Creative Training Techniques Newsletter in Action.*

A free catalog is available by calling 800-383-9210 (in the U.S.) or 612-829-1954.